The
SACRED
GIFT *of*
CHILDBIRTH

**MAKING
EMPOWERED
CHOICES
for YOU *and*
YOUR BABY**

The SACRED GIFT *of* CHILDBIRTH

MARIE-ANGE BIGELOW

CFI
An Imprint of Cedar Fort, Inc.
Springville, Utah

ISBN 13: 978-1-4621-1811-3

Published by CFI, an imprint of Cedar Fort, Inc.
2373 W. 700 S., Springville, UT 84663
Distributed by Cedar Fort, Inc., www.cedarfort.com

LIBRARY OF CONGRESS CATALOGING-IN-PUBLICATION DATA ON FILE

Cover design by Shawnda T. Craig
Cover design © 2016 by Cedar Fort, Inc.
Edited by Sydnee Hyer
Typeset by Rebecca Bird

Printed in the United States of America

10 9 8 7 6 5 4 3 2 1

Printed on acid-free paper

CONTENTS

CONTENTS

A Letter to the Reader

Dear Reader,

This book is my gift to you. I feel it is the greatest gift I can offer this world, aside from raising my children in the gospel. I have written it because of the many misconceptions about birth, its safety, and its impact on women and children. While our children are the greatest blessings we receive from giving birth, a woman can attain many other blessings from this experience—blessings that go unnoticed and often unreceived.

The events that bring a child into the world are sacred and purposeful. They are designed by a loving Heavenly Father who has entrusted women with the responsibility of bringing His spirit children into the world. This responsibility is an honor and a blessing. When a woman understands this privilege and sees Heavenly Father's hand in childbirth, she can find joy, strength, and faith through this experience.

Over the last century, secular and scientific influences have changed the childbirth experience of millions of women, particularly women in industrialized countries. In some ways, more thorough scientific knowledge has been helpful and has saved many lives. But these influences have also de-emphasized the sacredness of birth and removed most of the natural benefits that women were designed to experience during and after birth.

As a mother, I have been blessed with the beautiful births of my four children. As a doula (a specialist hired by an expectant couple to provide physical, emotional, and informational support during late pregnancy and childbirth), I have supported over one hundred couples during their births. I have also taught hundreds of couples in my childbirth education classes. I feel that my testimony of God's love for me has been integral in helping me understand the spiritual aspect of giving birth, and my education has provided me with a scientific understanding of birth. Both aspects—the spiritual and the physical—work together to provide women with a unique experience to not only become a mother, but to also grow spiritually and experience many blessings bestowed by a loving Heavenly Father.

I spent several years pondering and researching while I wrote this book. I understand that giving birth is not only sacred but also intimate and private. The way that you give birth is a personal decision, and knowing that you have chosen my writings as a way to help you make your birth decisions is not a responsibility I take lightly. I desire to pass on information that is valuable, beneficial, inspiring, and helpful to LDS mothers.

The information I pass on to you is evidence based, meaning that many scientific studies have come to the same conclusion and is scientifically regarded as truth. I will also share insights from my own experiences of giving birth, as well as years of experience working with a variety of couples while they prepared for and experienced their own births. I hope this book opens your eyes to the possibilities of birth and the wonders of Heavenly Father's plan for us—specifically the divine design of childbirth. I also hope it helps you view childbirth as a positive experience.

While I feel that all women can benefit from understanding God's plan for childbirth, this book is written with low-risk, healthy women in mind. This manuscript addresses childbirth as a whole, not on a case-by-case basis. Along with your trusted midwife or obstetrician, your personal beliefs regarding childbirth, and your own personal revelation, this manuscript will help you navigate your own birthing experience.

Upon finishing this book, you should not only have a true understanding of childbirth but also an idea of what type of birth will be most satisfying for you. You will know what current research has proven about common interventions, and you will know how to make safe and inspired choices concerning your own birth. Most important, you will know of God's love for you and trust that He will guide and strengthen you through this experience.

Marie

INTRODUCTION

*D*ecember 8, 2004. I will never forget that day or the night that preceded it. I had just tucked myself into bed after enjoying a creamy bowl of oatmeal and raisins. It was my latest craving during my first pregnancy, and I was glad that it was a healthy one (unlike the buffalo wing craving I would have with my next two pregnancies). I was somewhere between being asleep and awake when I began to feel very warm and wet. My water had broken in a large gush, and it didn't subside. I ran to the bathroom, leaving a trail of amniotic fluid behind me. My husband kept asking me if I was positive that my water had broken, almost as if a part of him didn't believe it. Or maybe his nerves didn't want him to believe it. He was so nervous. He showed me his shaking hands, and I told him he needed to get himself together because I was really going to need him that night. We gathered our last few toiletries, paused for a priesthood blessing, and got in the car to begin our drive to the hospital.

We lived in Logan, Utah, and were enjoying a midnight snowstorm. Homes sparkled with Christmas lights, and excitement filled the frozen air. It was also extremely cold! Amniotic fluid continued to run down my legs and even froze onto them (that was an unexpected surprise) as we walked through the icy parking lot into the hospital. After getting settled into our room, we called our parents, our doula, and my twin sister. My contractions were few and far between, so I took a few minutes to fix my hair and makeup. For some reason, I actually thought that it would make a difference with how I would look in the long run! It was so exciting.

After being a doula myself for a year, it was now my turn to give birth and my turn to have a doula.

Several hours later, most of my excitement had worn off. I had been dilated to four centimeters for three hours and counting, and our doula hadn't arrived yet due to the horrible weather. My husband and I were doing everything we were supposed to do—walking and moving, listening to music and relaxing—but I was really starting to wonder if this was a mountain I could climb. I kept having internal conversations with myself, debating over receiving some sort of pain medication, and wondering if I had picked the right profession. The only words I could verbalize were, "I don't know about this . . ." Over and over I uttered that phrase between contractions. I remember my husband looking at me, not quite knowing how to react. I'm sure he was starting to have similar doubts.

Our daughter's heart rate was decelerating instead of accelerating during contractions, so I was given a telemetry-monitoring unit to track her heart rate and allow me to move freely. Our nurse began to wonder if the cord was wrapped around our daughter's neck. We worked to find positions that proved to lessen the stress for her. And while I worried about my ability to cope with the pain, I believed that a natural delivery would be the safest way for me to bring her into the world.

Finally, things intensified quickly—almost too quickly! Thankfully our doula had arrived safely by this point. Within minutes I was dilated to eight centimeters and already had an urge to push. My doula guided me through breathing patterns designed to prevent a woman from pushing too soon. I was invigorated. I was at an eight! I *could* do it! It was almost over. Forty minutes later my daughter arrived. The cord was, indeed, wrapped around her neck, and it felt like she took forever to cry. (But once she started, she didn't stop for about six months!)[1]

After the routine weighing and measuring, Bronwyn-Rose and I were reunited. She was tiny—only six pounds, thirteen ounces. She was perfect and beautiful, and definitely ready for her first meal. She nursed perfectly for almost an hour. We listened to sweet lullabies as my husband and I spent our first few moments together as parents.

There is no way to fully describe the way I felt after I had given birth. Never before had I been so tired, hungry, sore, sublimely happy, and exhilarated all at the same time. I had never nursed a baby before, but it felt like the most important thing I had ever done. What I had accomplished in the last nine hours trumped every award, scholarship, and recognition I had ever received. I was on top of the world. My baby was here and in my arms! She was healthy and beautiful. I was a mommy, and my husband, a daddy. I had achieved the birth I desired, and that achievement continues to bless me physically, emotionally, and spiritually.

Things that I once felt were extremely important seemed to not matter at all anymore. It didn't matter that my husband and I were barely making enough to pay the bills. Or that we had been up all night and that my husband was missing class as he took our daughter to the nursery for her first bath. It didn't matter that I had sweated off every last grain of powder I had applied during early labor. All that mattered was a tiny baby in a small hospital room in a small town on a snowy morning.

Up to that point in my life, giving birth was easily the hardest thing I had ever done. Not only did I have to find the physical strength to endure to the end, but I also had to dig deep to find emotional and spiritual strength I didn't know I had. During my labor I frequently doubted myself. I felt the trial was too hard. I remember my doula telling me to stop fighting against my labor and to let myself surrender to it. Once I surrendered myself to the experience, thinking of it as God's will, I was able to find the power within to overcome. I left that experience a new being. I had transitioned from a pregnant woman to a mother. My testimony of God's love for me and my divine call to give birth had grown. My love for my husband had grown, and my love for my child had been etched into every cell of my body. I left that experience knowing that I wasn't just *willing* to do anything for my daughter; I was capable too.

My story is a stark contrast to many women's experience. My research and experience have convinced me that one of the most important things that made my birth such a triumph and positive experience was my decision to have a natural birth.

In spite of birth being such an important life event, many people are reluctant to speak about it or view it as such. I was surprised at many of the reactions I got after sharing my birth story with others. Most listeners wanted to know how much she weighed and what we named her, but few cared about what I had gone through to get her here. Several even put me down for choosing a natural birth. I wondered why and began to ponder what I could do to share my story in a way that would affect people positively.

Years have passed since that snowy night. But my passion for birth has only grown as I have taught childbirth education classes and attended births as a doula. Although I feel I have made a positive impact on hundreds of births, I have not been able to share the full truth with most of the couples with whom I work; without the gospel, couples are only getting a portion of the truth. As members of The Church of Jesus Christ of Latter-day Saints, our deeper understanding of God's creation and our role as women and mothers can have a positive influence on our birthing experiences and choices.

In her talk "Mothers Who Know," Julie B. Beck said, "Mothers who know desire to bear children."[2] While not referencing how to give birth, I believe her words encompass not only the desire to bear children but also the desire to understand childbirth and give birth safely. However, it often appears that the desire to bear children doesn't always lead to the desire to know *how* to bear them. Too many women do not understand the powerful impact bearing our children can have on our lives. Women today don't *know* birth.

I believe that if women today did know birth, they would have faith in it. They would know that labor and delivery are designed by God and designed to work. They would know that childbirth was created not only to bring their children to the world but also to bring them closer to God, closer to their spouse, and closer to their children.

We know that God designed the female body, and an integral part of that design was the ability to give birth. As difficult and trying as birth may be, it can be one of the most rewarding, empowering, humbling, exciting, edifying, uplifting, and amazing experiences in a woman's life.

Richard G. Scott taught, "Truth is the only meaningful foundation upon which we can make wise decisions."[3] We can easily apply this counsel to giving birth, as childbirth requires us to make many important decisions. Couples simply cannot make wise birth choices without understanding the physical, physiological, *and* spiritual aspects of birth. Due to lack of education, many couples are left confused, discouraged, and disenchanted when they return home from a stressful birthing experience.

My goal is to educate couples so they can make well-informed evidence-based decisions and also have the calming reassurance of the Holy Ghost. You don't need to become a birthing expert to make wise decisions, but you do need a certain amount of knowledge to make responsible decisions.

The goal of this book is to take what has been proven scientifically about birth and combine it with spiritual truths about family and motherhood so expectant couples can understand the full truth about birth. In turn, couples can then rely on the Lord to assist them during their births, strengthen and magnify their abilities, and help them know which decisions will be safest and most rewarding for their particular birth.

So what *is* the truth about birth? I will discuss the following truths in this book:

- Childbirth is a blessing, not a curse.

- Heavenly Father designed birth as a safe way to bring spirits to earth.

- Childbirth physiologically prepares a woman to love her child intensely.

- Natural childbirth is the safest way to give birth in low-risk situations.

- Breastfeeding strengthens the mother-infant bond and provides the infant with physical protection against illness.

- God magnifies the birthing woman.

- Medical intervention is needed at times, but the overuse of those interventions makes birth more harmful.

- Birth affects women emotionally.

- Fathers have a strong influence on the birthing experience and must protect their families during this vulnerable time.

- By partnering with God in creation, you get a small glimpse into godhood.

These truths can not only help you give birth safely, but they can also enable you to strengthen your testimony, feel closer to your Heavenly Father, and inspire you to view birth as a sacred and holy event.

NOTES

1. Cords often wrap around infants' necks in utero and hardly ever cause distress to the infant. My situation was rare. The majority of the time, this does not cause difficulties for the birth.
2. Julie B. Beck, "Mothers Who Know," *Ensign*, November 2007.
3. Richard G. Scott, "Truth: 'The Foundation of Correct Decisions,'" *Ensign*, November 2007.

Helpful Terminology

Vaginal birth: Any birth that is not a cesarean. A vaginal birth can be natural or medical.

Natural birth: A birth that occurs completely naturally, meaning it starts on its own and has no medical interventions.

Medical birth: A birth that has either been induced or has some sort of pharmacological pain management, or both.

Assisted or **Instrumental Delivery:** A vaginal birth that is assisted with the use of a vacuum or forceps.

Pathology: The study of disease. In maternity care, pathology is anything that is unhealthy or unsafe to the mother or child. Anything that is included under high-risk is pathology.

Low-Risk: A pregnancy that does not have any signs of pathology. A low-risk patient is expected to have a labor that progresses safely and normally, and does not have any "red flags" before labor begins. The overwhelming majority of women fit into this category.

High-Risk: A pregnancy that has certain "red flags" (such as gestational diabetes, high blood pressure, previous stillbirth) that would lead a care provider to believe that a vaginal birth has a greater chance of requiring medical interventions. However, many high-risk patients go on to have natural births.

Evidence-Based: Based on current research and proven to be most effective and safe through controlled, scientific studies.

Morbidity: Illness or injury that is a direct result of childbirth. Some examples are episiotomy, infection, and pelvic trauma.

Mortality: The death of a mother or child during or directly after childbirth.

Hormones: Chemical messengers inside our bodies that greatly influence critical processes in our lives, including our growth and development, metabolism, moods, sex drives, menstruation, fertility, pregnancy, and birth. This book talks in detail about the hormones associated with pregnancy and birth, particularly oxytocin and estrogen.

Colostrum: The first milk a mother produces. Colostrum is low in volume but high in fat and antibodies. Colostrum is replaced with breast milk several days after birth.

Lactogenesis: The process of the mother's milk coming in.

Section One

GOD'S PLAN FOR BIRTH

*B*efore deciding what type of birth you desire, it is important to understand childbirth from a physical, physiological, and spiritual perspective. This section will walk you through each of those areas so you can truly understand that God had a plan and a purpose for every aspect of labor and birth. You will learn how the female body gives birth, and why birth unfolds the way it does.

"The first commandment that God gave to Adam and Eve pertained to their potential for parenthood as husband and wife. We declare that God's commandment for His children to multiply and replenish the earth remains in force."[1]

The Family: A Proclamation to the World

Chapter 1

CHILDBIRTH IS A BLESSING, NOT A CURSE

*C*hildbirth—It is the literal passageway from God's presence to earthly life. Without it, there could be no plan of happiness, no families, no mortal bodies. The gift of childbirth enables us to gain an earthly body in order to become like our Heavenly Parents. Woman's ability to bear children is key to God's plan and key to our eternal salvation.

This pure and simple doctrine is taught in the Primary song "The Family Is of God": "Our Father has a family. It's me! It's you, all others too: we are His children. He sent each one of us to earth, through birth, To live and learn here in families."[2]

It is through birth, and because of birth, that mortal life can take place. Though childbirth is sacred, popular culture and society often do not view it as such. Many religions teach that childbirth is a curse placed on women, and many women fear giving birth. An event that should be celebrated with gratitude and joy is devalued, distorted, and even dreaded.

Shortly before having my third child, I attended a Lamaze childbirth education seminar. Not only did I learn valuable skills to improve my teaching as a childbirth educator, but I was also able to spend three days with women who are as passionate about birth as I am. Because I am part of a small, birth-loving minority, a weekend like that was pretty spectacular. Like all women who have given birth do, we shared our own birth stories with each other during our breaks.

A young mother who had recently given birth shared with me the feelings she had during the transition stage of her labor (when the cervix dilates from eight to ten centimeters, often the most difficult and intense part of labor). She said something along the lines of, "I just kept asking God why He made it so bad—why He had to punish us so horribly." She was not a member of our faith but was a devout Christian with wonderful values. Her perspective of birth as a punishment saddened me. Knowing that this woman did not have the added understanding of the Fall available because of the Restoration of the gospel, I wasn't surprised to hear her assessment of birth. But still, it was disheartening to me that someone who loved Christ dearly and also believed strongly in the benefits of natural childbirth could believe that birth was a punishment placed on women. I told her that I believed childbirth was divinely designed by a *loving* Heavenly Father, who created childbirth for our benefit, not our punishment. She gave me something of a strange look when I was finished (as did several other women who couldn't help but overhear). Then she said something like, "I've never looked at it that way," and the subject quickly changed.

When glancing through scriptural passages related to Eve, it is easy to see how childbirth can be viewed negatively. At first read, it can seem like childbirth is a punishment. But when we study and ponder the scriptures and combine them with revelation from modern-day prophets, we see that birth is for our benefit.

Because of the following verses in Genesis, women for centuries have viewed birth as a punishment: "Unto the woman he said, I will greatly multiply thy sorrow and thy conception; in sorrow thou shalt bring forth children; and thy desire shall be to thy husband, and he shall rule over thee. And unto Adam he said, Because thou hast hearkened unto the voice of thy wife, and hast eaten of the tree, of which I commanded thee, saying, Thou shalt not eat of it: cursed is the ground for thy sake; in sorrow shalt thou eat of it all the days of thy life" (Genesis 3:16–17).

These verses do make it sound like birth is something we are doomed to endure, all because of Eve's curiosity. Sadly, this belief has prompted women to view childbirth in a negative light.

A correct understanding of the Fall in a spiritual sense is the first step in understanding our heavenly and earthly role as women. In "The Family: A Proclamation to the World" we learn that "gender is an essential characteristic of individual premortal, mortal, and eternal identity and purpose."[3] If we believe that childbirth was a punishment placed upon women *because* Eve partook of the fruit, then we can't believe that God had already determined gender roles—they were determined because of Eve's actions. But from this one statement we know that gender and gender roles were determined long before Adam and Eve were ever placed in the Garden of Eden. All the women who have ever lived and who will ever live on the earth were women in the premortal world. We understood that we had been chosen to bear children when we chose to follow Heavenly Father's plan of happiness. And we *still* chose to come to earth, so it couldn't have seemed all that bad!

Our gender and accompanying gender roles were determined well before the Garden of Eden, but it wasn't until after the Fall that either sex could reach their potential and accomplish what God had required. After the Fall, no one was punished. We were all extremely blessed to gain an earthly body and to accomplish with our bodies that which would some-day lead us back to God's presence.

M. Russell Ballard further explains this concept: "As the proclama-tion clearly states, men and women, though spiritually equal, are entrusted with different but equally significant roles. These roles complement each other. Men are given stewardship over the sacred ordinances of the priest-hood. To women, God gives stewardship over bestowing and nurturing mortal life, including providing physical bodies for God's spirit children and guiding those children toward a knowledge of gospel truths."[4]

The Family Proclamation also states, "The first commandment that God gave to Adam and Eve pertained to their potential for parenthood as husband and wife. We declare that God's commandment for His children to multiply and replenish the earth remains in force."[5] I cannot believe that the first commandment given to Adam and Eve was also a punish-ment. Would a loving Heavenly Father really expect almost all the women in the world to suffer just because of Eve? No. Jesus suffered for our sins, and we are not to be punished for Adam's transgression (Articles of Faith 1:2). Dallin H. Oaks said, "It was Eve who first transgressed the limits of Eden in order to initiate the conditions of mortality. Her act, whatever its nature, was formally a transgression but eternally a glorious necessity to open the doorway toward eternal life. Adam showed his wisdom by doing the same. . . . We celebrate Eve's act and honor her wisdom and courage in the great episode called the Fall."[6]

The *Old Testament Gospel Doctrine Teacher's Manual* emphasizes how the Fall of Adam and Eve benefits us, and explains that we all inher-ited the consequences of the Fall, but not the responsibility of it.[7] We know that Eve's decision to eat the forbidden fruit was key to God's plan. Imagine our joy as we learned that mortal life would soon begin and our natural desire to bear and nurture children would soon be fulfilled in a mortal realm.

We know that all commandments given to us are for our protection, growth, and refinement. Of course multiplying and replenishing the earth encompass much more than just the delivery of the child, but labor and delivery play a key part that is all too often overlooked and underappreciated. A woman's experience during labor and delivery changes her forever—physically, chemically, biologically, and emotionally.

The use of the word *sorrow* causes many to view womanhood, and the act of bearing children, as a punishment. Few take the time to notice that Adam himself was also doomed to sorrow and that even the land was cursed. In these two verses, *sorrow* describes the new circumstances that Adam and Eve would enter. Initially, it was most likely devastating to be removed from the Garden of Eden and enter into a world with opposition. Trees would no longer bear fruit effortlessly. Adam and Eve now experienced new emotions of shame and embarrassment. Adam would have to learn to prepare the soil and skillfully prune and maintain the trees. Work would be essential. Therefore, sorrow was the introduction of the opposition in all things and was essential for mortals to truly understand joy. Some of our greatest moments of pride and accomplishment come after we have worked hard for something. God was now insisting that Adam and Eve work, which in turn would bring them far more joy than the Garden of Eden ever could.

President Ezra Taft Benson said, "The earth was cursed for Adam's sake. Work is our blessing, not our doom. God has a work to do, and so should we."[8]

Growth comes through hard work, and working hard is a good thing. While it is easy to doubt yourself, you *can* do hard things. But why does childbirth have to involve so *much* hard work? Surely if giving birth were easy and painless, no one would confuse it with being a curse. With all of His power and ability, couldn't God have created a way to give birth that wasn't so painful? Yes, He could have created it any way He saw fit. So there must be a reason He chose not to.

Consider three possible reasons for the pain in childbirth: First, there must be opposition in all things. Second, the pain of childbirth molds and refines women as they transition into motherhood. By experiencing the pain of childbirth, they have a deeper understanding of and gratitude for Christ's suffering for them, which helps them become more like Him. Third, the pain communicates to the mother that birth is imminent.

OPPOSITION

In 2 Nephi, Lehi teaches his family the importance of opposition in all things:

"For it must needs be, that there is an opposition in all things. If not so, my firstborn in the wilderness, righteousness could not be brought to pass, neither wickedness, neither holiness nor misery, neither good nor bad. Wherefore, all things must needs be a compound in one; wherefore, if it should be one body it must needs remain as dead, having no life neither death, nor corruption nor incorruption, happiness nor misery, neither sense nor insensibility" (2 Nephi 2:11).

Some of the most meaningful events in our life will be full of opposition. This is partly what will give those events their great meaning. While I believe in natural childbirth and encourage all low-risk women to have this as a goal, I will never say that it is easy. Pregnancy and birth are full of opposition. But it is *because* of this opposition that we are able to experience the full spectrum of joy surrounding the birth of our children.

LEARNING ABOUT THE ATONEMENT

Childbirth gives women a unique and edifying opportunity to learn more about the Atonement. Because of His love for us, Christ was willing to experience an unfathomable pain. Similar to Christ, mothers are willing to drink the bitter cup and experience pain (though in a *much* smaller magnitude than the burden Christ shouldered) in order to serve someone they love. Mothers can have a new understanding of Christ's words in Luke 22:42: "Father, if thou be willing, remove this cup from me: nevertheless not my will, but thine, be done."

During childbirth, a woman may experience similar feelings. She may wish for her labor to be somehow taken away from her, but she will have to surrender to God's will. But just as Christ was resurrected and was made whole after His suffering in the garden and on the cross, we too are made whole: our bodies heal, and after our travail we often find that our capacity to love and serve has increased. Our gratitude to Jesus has grown, as we now have been able to see a small glimpse into what the Atonement was like for Him.

The Atonement and childbirth are both examples of a purposeful pain that brings to pass something remarkable. And as there is no other way to return to Heavenly Father's presence than through the Atonement, there is no other way to bring mortals to the world than through the love of a mother.

Like the Atonement, the process of giving birth can be a healing experience. I meet with all of my doula clients approximately two weeks after they give birth. The purpose of this visit is to assess for postpartum depression, determine how well breastfeeding is going, and to discuss the birth. A particular client expressed to me how she felt her birth had been a healing event in her life. She had a difficult childhood, especially after her parents divorced, had struggled within her own marriage, and felt that during her first two births she had not been treated well by the staff who were assigned to her birth. She also received an injury from her epidural and felt that she never fully regained strength in certain muscles. Her third pregnancy was unplanned and had caused much stress. She knew she needed to have a different birthing experience this time. She opted for midwifery care in a birthing center and hired me as her doula.

Her birth was incredible. She remained peaceful throughout, and labor progressed without any concerns. It was her only time giving birth naturally. Within minutes of giving birth, she said that the entire pregnancy was worth experiencing such a wonderful birth. She particularly pointed out that she had never felt so valued and supported during a birth (this is key to most women whether they opt for a natural birth or not). Again, at her postpartum visit she expressed similar feelings and told me how she felt the amazing experience of her birth had made up for struggles and pain she experienced in the past. She truly felt God had given her the gift of this birth to heal her heart. Imagine how different the world would be if every woman felt this way after giving birth.

Birth Is Imminent

Pain is also a way that our bodies communicate with our brains. Pain tells us to quickly remove our hand from a hot surface. Prolonged or intense pain tells us that we may have a serious injury or illness. Pain is often the first or only symptom people experience before being diagnosed with myriad health concerns. Until the days of elective inductions and cesareans, the day a baby decided to be born was a mystery for all expectant women. Though we cannot predict the day labor will begin, we definitely need to know when the birth will take place. And pain tells us just that.

As our contractions become longer, stronger, and closer together, we become more aware that birth is imminent. The hardship of contractions forces us to focus on our labor and prepare to take care of our child.

Obviously, the pain we experience in childbirth is what makes childbirth difficult. It makes us doubt ourselves. It evokes fear in many women. And why wouldn't it? We've gone our whole lives knowing that pain means something is wrong! But once you have experienced the opposition of birth (or the pain), it seems like a small inconvenience to be where you are after. Pain no longer matters once you have your child in your arms. The scriptures even speak of this:

"Verily, verily, I say unto you, That ye shall weep and lament, but the world shall rejoice: and ye shall be sorrowful, but your sorrow shall be turned into joy.

"A woman when she is in travail hath sorrow, because her hour is come: but as soon as she is delivered of the child, she remembereth no more the anguish, for joy that a man is born into the world" (John 16:20–21).

The way a woman views labor and its accompanying pain will, in large part, determine if she feels it is a blessing or a curse. Choose to be thankful for the miraculous way Eve's choice has blessed your life. Remember her wisdom in knowing that by partaking of the fruit, she would become more like God. Calling childbirth a punishment couldn't be further from the truth.

Notes

1. "The Family: A Proclamation to the World," *Ensign*, November 1995, 102.
2. Matthew Neeley, "The Family Is of God," *Friend*, October 2008.
3. "The Family: A Proclamation."
4. M. Russell Ballard, "The Sacred Responsibility of Parenthood," from an Education Week devotional address given on August 19, 2003, at Brigham Young University.
5. "The Family: A Proclamation."
6. Dallin H. Oaks, "The Great Plan of Happiness," *Ensign*, November 1993.
7. "Lesson 4: Because of My Transgression My Eyes are Opened," *Old Testament: Gospel Doctrine Teacher's Manual*, 2001, 12–16.
8. Ezra Taft Benson, "Do Not Despair," *Ensign*, November 1974.

"*Woman has filled a wonderful part in the march of progress, but most important of all the duties that have been laid upon the gentler sex, is the duty of bringing into the world and rearing, the children of our Heavenly Father.*"[1]

George Albert Smith

Chapter 2

HOW GOD DESIGNED BIRTH

*I*n 2003, one of my closest friends, Nicki, became a mother. She was the first from my circle of friends to reach this milestone, and her journey fascinated me. She called me the morning after her birth. "I had my baby last night, and I did it all natural!" I was thrilled for her. I knew that she strongly desired a natural birth. At this point in my life, Nicki was the only woman I knew who had given birth without an epidural.

Nicki and I worked together in the music therapy office at Utah State University and spent hours talking together. Over the months, I had watched in amazement as my tiny friend grew an enormous belly. When her baby would kick, she would grab my hand and let me feel. It was so odd. I had never been close to a pregnant woman before. And even though I was newly married, I hadn't thought much about getting pregnant myself. Nicki began reading many books about pregnancy and childbirth. After her own personal study, she began to understand the benefits of a natural delivery and aspired to experience one. The topic of natural childbirth consumed most of our conversations, as both of us felt compelled to study and learn more.

Within months of her baby's birth, both she and I attended a training to become professional doulas. At this point, the only thing I knew about birth was that I *had* to learn more. I had never had such a strong desire to learn about something.

Even though I felt called to this line of work, I was completely unprepared for the training. I had never been involved in a birth, and I knew very little about the topic. I had the typical reactions you would expect from an unprepared young woman watching a birth for the first time on an enormous TV. I felt awkward. It felt really strange to watch a naked woman. I was completely unaware of afterbirth and had no idea what a placenta looked like. There was a huge learning curve. I was the only woman there who hadn't given birth, and it was obvious!

We watched dozens of births that weekend. While they all ended with the birth of a child, each birth was unique and had varying obstacles for each laboring mom. At first I was watching to learn. I really tried to understand what was going on, what the woman was experiencing, and what I could do as a doula to support a woman in that situation.

Throughout the training, my response to watching birth changed. It wasn't about nudity, pain, or blood anymore. It was about life. About love. About God. While birth appeared to be a physical event, I found the training to be extremely spiritual as well. I felt the Spirit often, and I found my testimony of motherhood and family strengthened as I studied.

I learned that God has created our bodies to give birth. Our brains and our wombs are designed to work together in harmony to create a safe passageway into earthly life.

When trying to understand birth, it is of the utmost importance to remember that everything about pregnancy, labor, delivery, and newborn care was created by a loving Heavenly Father who knows what is best for you and your baby. While there will always be exceptions, we can safely assume that God's original design is what will work best for the general population.

How God Designed Birth

There are two processes that take place during the birth of a child. The first, and more widely known, is the physical process, during which the uterus contracts, the cervix opens up to ten centimeters, and the baby descends through the birth canal until it is born. The second, and lesser known, is the physiological process that occurs in the brain. This process not only orchestrates the labor but also ensures that once a woman has given birth that she is flooded with feelings of joy, love, and maternal instincts. The physical process ensures the birth of the child, and the physiological process ensures the birth of a mother.

Physical Aspects of Labor and Birth

Childbirth can be broken down into three stages:[2]

Stage 1: Labor—The process that dilates a woman's cervix to ten centimeters.

Stage 2: Pushing—The period of time when the woman begins pushing until her baby is born.

Stage 3: After-birth—The delivery of the placenta several minutes after the baby is born. When this happens, childbirth is complete.

Stage 1 (labor) can be broken down into three phases: (1) early labor, (2) active labor, and (3) transition.

Early labor occurs when a woman's cervix dilates from zero to four or five centimeters. Current researchers even speculate that early labor lasts until a woman is dilated to six centimeters.[3] Early labor contractions are mild, and at the beginning can be as much as twenty minutes apart and last only thirty seconds. Over time, contractions grow closer together and become stronger. Most of early labor is easy to cope with. Many women can function normally. Most women find it difficult to determine when early labor actually begins. Some will even feel that early labor symptoms lasted for several days before the birth. At the end of early labor, contractions are consistently six or seven minutes apart. (Contractions are timed from the beginning of one contraction to the beginning of the next contraction. Many couples try to time the space in between contractions, but that is not the correct way to time them.)

Active labor begins when the cervix dilates from about five centimeters to eight centimeters. The mother is no longer able to function normally, and all of her attention is focused on getting through her contractions. Her contractions last about forty-five to sixty seconds and are about five minutes apart. The length of labor varies greatly from woman to woman, but it is typically longer in first-time moms. Active labor can last anywhere from four to twelve hours for first-time moms. It's important to remember that laboring mothers are *not* contracting for the majority of the time. About 20 percent of active labor is spent having contractions. The other 80 percent is typically free of discomfort and allows mom time to rest and refocus.

Transition occurs when the cervix dilates from eight to ten centimeters. Transition can be intense, as contractions last sixty to ninety seconds and are only two to three minutes apart. It is the only time during the labor that the uterus is contracting more than it is resting. Thankfully, transition is the shortest phase of labor and is typically around two hours for a first-time mom. For women who have already given birth, transition can be just a handful of contractions.

Contractions cause the cervix to dilate (open) and efface (thin) and then push the baby into the birth canal. Once the head is low enough to put pressure on the woman's rectal nerves, she will experience a strong urge to push her baby out. Strong contractions will continue until the birth of her child; then milder contractions continue until the placenta is also expelled. Contractions will come and go for several days after the birth. These contractions are important because they help the uterus return to its normal size and prevent hemorrhage. These contractions, also called after-pains, tend to become more painful with each birth.

PHYSIOLOGICAL ASPECTS OF LABOR AND BIRTH

The physiological side of labor is the orchestration of hormones and endorphins that start labor, keep labor progressing, raise the woman's pain tolerance, and promote bonding. It all begins and ends with the hormone called oxytocin. Outside of childbirth, oxytocin is the hormone of love and bonding and is associated with long-term, loving relationships. During childbirth, oxytocin tells the mother's brain to love, protect, and nurture her infant, and also tells the uterus to contract and labor to begin.

When the brain releases oxytocin into the mother's bloodstream during labor, it assists in stimulating contractions. Contractions cause the woman's cervix to dilate and efface, allowing the baby to descend into the birth canal. The more oxytocin that is released, the stronger and more frequent the contractions become. During each contraction, the laboring woman will have a small oxytocin rush, training her to love and protect her infant while she labors.[4]

In response to the discomfort of contractions, the woman's brain secretes powerful endorphins, which raise her pain tolerance level *higher than it has ever been before*. These endorphins also help her remain calm and alert, even when labor is long and tiring.[5] This continues until she is ready to begin pushing, when a burst of adrenaline gives her body the energy it needs to deliver her baby.[6] But it doesn't stop there. Something completely miraculous happens at the moment of birth (aside from the birth itself). At the moment of birth, the mother's brain releases more oxytocin and endorphins *than at any other time* in her life.[7] High amounts of endorphins after birth make a mother feel euphoric and ecstatic, similar to how a runner feels after completing a marathon, and the peak of oxytocin floods the mother's brain with feelings of intense love and maternal instincts.[8]

The hormone estrogen, which is greatly increased during pregnancy, causes the mother's brain to produce more oxytocin receptors, making her even more responsive to the flood of oxytocin after birth. These receptors are found in the part of the brain that promotes maternal behavior. The mother's oxytocin affects her child's production of oxytocin and trains their brains to prefer each other's smell. This flood of oxytocin also influences maternal behavior during the initial breastfeeding session and helps make nursing feel more natural to the inexperienced mother.[9] This physiological firework session helps a woman instantly bond to her baby and find great joy in being close to her child and meeting his or her needs.

While a scientific understanding of the birth high is helpful, the best way to conceptualize it is to hear from women who have experienced it. Below are the stories of two mothers who felt the birth high.

Ginny said:

> The afterbirth surge of love is impossible to describe adequately. It feels like coming home, being wrapped in a million loving embraces that sink through the flesh and embrace at the very heart of the soul. All that I had just gone through was worth it for that reward! I was filled with strength of will and spirit in that time, given confidence not my own, and a very specific connection to heaven on behalf of this, my firstborn child. I have since given birth three more times naturally, as well as had a natural stillborn birth. Each time intense love for my darling baby and from my heavenly ancestors filled me up and gave me courage and strength I did not have before. I could not ever be the same. I could not see birth as something frightening or dangerous; it was sacred and spiritual.[10]

Emmy said:

> As soon as my daughter was born, all the intensity of labor was taken away and replaced by total relief, peacefulness, excitement, and love. After an hour of skin-to-skin time and breastfeeding, the evening faded and our house grew quiet. My husband was flopped out next to me, rhythmically snoring. Our dimly lit room left a warm glow over

the profile of my fresh little baby's face swaddled into her nest next to me. My body was tired from walking several miles and THEN working to birth a baby, but I felt incredible. It felt great to lie back in my soft bed while gazing into the crook of my arm at our new baby!

I spent the entire first night of Josie's existence watching her sleep, tending to her few diapers and nursing sessions, and staring at our wall—HA! I tried closing my eyes many times to sleep, but my brain was BUZZING. Like a favorite movie, my mind played her birth over and over in the hours that followed, skipping past the slower parts and savoring the moments where I felt most powerful and in awe. I knew this time would come to an end all too soon.

Many women have told me their favorite part of labor was when "it was over and I had a baby in my arms." I totally agree with what they are saying—labor is hard work and the big reward for your work is getting to hold that baby for the first time. But for me, my favorite part of the process of giving birth is the full twenty-four hours AFTER birth. . . . My body feels alive and clean and STRONG, and my mind is alert and present. I have experienced this feeling four times (soon to be five!), and I can absolutely say, there is NOTHING in life that can compare. It truly is a birth high![11]

BREASTFEEDING

Though not an official stage of labor, the first time the mother and infant breastfeed is the final step in giving birth. This first feed signifies the infant's well-being and ability to thrive outside of the womb. Timely breastfeeding is also in the mother's best interest because nursing will continue to stimulate the production of oxytocin. This continual production will cause the woman's uterus to continue contracting, which helps the uterus return to its normal size and ensures that post-birth bleeding is minimal.[12]

During this time, mother and infant experience a symbiotic relationship, as breastfeeding promotes survival for both of them. Before medical intervention, breastfeeding was a woman's most important step in preventing post-birth hemorrhage, and it is still incredibly valuable to a woman's safety and well-being after giving birth.

Women who breastfeed produce more oxytocin and may spend more time holding their babies because they have a built-in reason to hold their baby throughout the day. This frequency of togetherness ensures a strong attachment. It is a fact known and even conceived by a loving God who surely wants you to experience the benefits of a lifetime rich with the love and lasting relationships oxytocin helps create.

The Physical–Physiological Connection

The entire scope of procreation is dependent upon the physical and physiological aspects of conception and birth. Though different physically, intercourse and childbirth are similar physiologically, as both experiences reach their full potential through high amounts of oxytocin. And while they both have a primary purpose of procreation, they also have the unique potential to strengthen our family relationships greatly.

Oxytocin causes butterflies in the beginning of a romantic relationship, increases during lovemaking, and spikes during sexual climax. Intimacy is reserved for marriage because sex brings you physically and physiologically closer to your spouse than any other person. Lovemaking, with the intent of meeting each other's physical and emotional needs, keeps spousal bonds tight. When you strengthen your marriage physically, you are physiologically coding your brain to love your husband.

This same type of love-coding occurs during labor, after birth, and during breastfeeding. As the physical and physiological aspects of our bodies work together, we are blessed with the opportunity to draw closer to our spouses, conceive and bear children, and raise those children with intense feelings of love for them and for our spouses. It is no coincidence that oxytocin is a key ingredient for intimacy, childbirth, and bonding.

Sex and birth can both occur physically without the physiological component. But it is the physiology of these two acts that give them their intense meaning and strong effect on long-term relationships. It is critical to understand that the physiological aspects of labor, birth, and initial breastfeeding are only seen in natural births and are greatly impeded when births are induced, managed with epidurals, or done via cesarean. All vaginal births will have the same physical aspects of labor, but the physiology will vary greatly depending on interventions used. Understanding and desiring the physiological benefits of natural birth can be a great motivator for many women preparing for a natural birth.

While there will always be inherent risks associated with giving birth, there is safety in God's design for birth, as natural birth provides the safest pathway to earth for low-risk situations. The physical and physiological components of birth work together to ensure that labor progresses safely for the mother and for the infant. Along with increased safety, natural childbirth can also provide a woman with many emotional and spiritual benefits. Understanding the safety of childbirth, and knowing of God's love for us, we can assume that His design was created to bless our lives greatly and trust that He will strengthen and enable those who desire this type of birth.

Physical Aspects of Labor and Birth	Physiological Aspects of (Natural) Labor and Birth
Contractions	Oxytocin production to stimulate contractions
Dilation of the cervix from 0 to 10 centimeters	Endorphin release to fight pain
Effacement of the cervix	Endorphin release to keep laboring mom
Descent of the baby into the birth canal	Calm and alert
Birth of the baby	Adrenaline rush to give mom needed energy boost for pushing
Delivery of the placenta	Oxytocin high after birth to promote heightened bonding and create intense feelings of love
	Heightened maternal instincts
	Endorphin high causing feelings of euphoria and extreme joy

Notes

1. George Albert Smith, "Women's Divine Roles and Responsibilities," *Eternal Marriage Student Manual*, 2003.

2. William and Martha Sears, *The Birth Book* (Massachusetts: Little, Brown and Company, 1994).

3. "Safe Prevention of the Primary Cesarean Delivery," *ACOG*, March 2014.

4. Sarah Buckley, "The Hidden Risks of Epidurals," *Mothering* No. 133, November–December 2005; Carol Sakala and Maureen P. Corry, *Evidence-*

Based Maternity Care: What It Is and What It Can Achieve (New York: Milbank Memorial Fund, 2008).

5. "Hormones Driving Labor and Birth," *Childbirth Connection*, April 2011.

6. Buckley, "The Hidden Risks of Epidurals"; Sakala and Corry, *Evidence-Based Maternity Care.*

7. Buckley, "The Hidden Risks of Epidurals."

8. "Hormones Driving Labor and Birth."

9. Linda Folden Palmer, "The Chemistry of Attachment," *The Attached Family*, http://theattachedfamily.com/?p=4979.

10. Personal correspondence with Ginny Ferguson.

11. Personal correspondence with Emmy Lay.

12. Sakala and Corry, *Evidence-Based Maternity Care*; Jeanette Crenshaw, "Lamaze Healthy Birth Practice #6: Keep Mother and Baby Together–It's Best for Mother, Baby, and Breastfeeding," *Lamaze International*, 2009.

"Mothers, cherish that role that is so uniquely yours and for which heaven itself sends angels to watch over you and your little ones. Yours is the work of salvation, and therefore you will be magnified, compensated, made more than you are, better than you are, and better than you have ever been. And if, for whatever reason, you are making this courageous effort alone, without your husband at your side, then our prayers will be all the greater for you. Know that in faith things will be made right in spite of you, or more correctly, because of you. We thank all of you, and tell you there is nothing more important in this world than participating so directly in the work and glory of God.

"May I say to mothers collectively, in the name of the Lord, you are magnificent. You are doing terrifically well. The very fact that you have been given such a responsibility is everlasting evidence of the trust your Father in Heaven has in you. He is blessing you and He will bless you, even—no, especially—when your days and your nights may be the most challenging. Rely on Him. Rely on Him heavily. Rely on Him forever. And 'press forward with a steadfastness in Christ, having a perfect brightness of hope.'"[1]

Jeffrey R. Holland

Chapter 3

THE MAGNIFICATION PROCESS

*T*he high use of birth interventions today sends a message to many women that we are not capable of giving birth without these interventions. In reality, we are very capable of doing so! The Lord has designed our bodies in a way that He can magnify them during pregnancy and childbirth. These changes help our bodies withstand much more than they can at other times.

As you recall from our previous discussion about the natural birth process, our brains secrete powerful endorphins during labor to greatly increase our pain tolerance. This is only one of the ways Heavenly Father strengthens us as we give birth. Our divinely designed bodies are also full of maternal instincts during this time and can literally guide themselves through childbirth.

In our modern day we can also magnify ourselves with scientific knowledge and by gaining an understanding of childbirth. Childbirth education, the support of a doula, and evidence-based medical care can magnify a modern woman and enable her to have the safest and most satisfying birth *ever* available.

MAGNIFICATION FROM A LOVING HEAVENLY FATHER

I don't want to go any further without acknowledging that natural birth is intimidating. Feelings of inadequacy will slip into the mind of even the most prepared parent. It is important for women desiring natural birth to always remember that God will magnify your abilities. We read

29

examples of the Lord magnifying his servants throughout the scriptures, and in 1 Nephi we can even learn of times when women were magnified during their birthing and early parenting experiences:

> And it came to pass that we did again take our journey in the wilderness: and we did travel nearly eastward from that time forth. And we did travel and wade through much affliction in the wilderness; and our women did bear children in the wilderness.
>
> And so great were the blessings of the Lord upon us, that while we did live upon raw meat in the wilderness, our women did give plenty of suck for their children, and were strong, yea, even like unto the men; and they began to bear their journeyings without murmurings.
>
> And thus we see that the commandments of God must be fulfilled. And if it so be that the children of men keep the commandments of God he doth nourish them, and strengthen them, and provide means whereby they can accomplish the thing which he has commanded them; wherefore, he did provide means for us while we did sojourn in the wilderness. (1 Nephi 17:1–3)

Giving birth is not a test designed to separate the weak from the strong. It is an opportunity for women to gain strength by receiving strength from the Lord. Now is the time to become a creative team with your Father in Heaven and put your faith and trust in Him and His almighty power. He created you. He loves you. And He *will* magnify you.

When I was in my late teen years, I was running around the house and laughing hysterically with my twin sister. I slipped and sharply hit my hip bone on a doorknob. Pain seared through me, and suddenly I blacked out. I woke up with half my body in my bedroom and the other half in the hallway. I started shaking uncontrollably. I was freezing; I was in shock. What does this have to do with anything? I experienced a reaction to pain. Real pain. I always explain to my clients that labor pain is not "real" pain.

In all aspects of your life, except for menstruation and childbirth, your body feels pain as a way to warn you that something is wrong. This relays information to yourself that you are in harm's way, and your body reacts appropriately. But during childbirth, your body does not react to the pain you are feeling in the same way. Labor pain does not raise your blood pressure, does not increase your heart rate, does not make you go into shock, and cannot harm you. During these times your body is actually telling you that you are experiencing a healthy part of female life, even though it can feel like harm. When you understand this, you realize that the pain we experience during childbirth is not the "real" pain that we typically experience, even though it may feel like it!

A doula client of mine found this explanation extremely helpful and even chanted, "It's not real," during her contractions. She had an amazing natural birth. By reframing her perception of labor pain and gaining an understanding of what was truly happening to her body, she was able to cope and overcome.

When we are in pain, we tend to become afraid. It is a natural response. This is why relaxation is a key component to a natural delivery. But fear makes us feel tense. This increases our perception of our pain and makes us feel even more pain and fear. In the birthing world, this is referred to as the fear-tension cycle. The spiral effect it causes can negatively influence your birth. Understanding that labor pain isn't a harmful pain, and knowing that God created us to withstand the pain of contractions, can have a wonderfully positive effect on our births.

During pregnancy a woman's pain tolerance is greatly increased as her hormones increase and prepare her for childbirth.[2] That is a how a girl who passed out from hitting her hip on a doorknob gave birth four times without pain medication. (Most of my friends were shocked when they heard I gave birth naturally!) This is a tender mercy from a loving Heavenly Father. He knew how difficult bearing children would be, so he created our bodies in a way that would naturally become stronger during our pregnancies and prepare us for giving birth. His hormonal design magnifies us to be stronger than we ever thought we could be.

Those desiring a natural birth must believe in their ability to give birth, and believe that God has created their body to do so. Remember that your body was created specifically with the ability to give birth. Also remember to have faith in the Lord and trust that He will magnify you and make up for your human weaknesses. Nephi set a wonderful example of this when he said, "And it came to pass that I, Nephi, said unto my father: I will go and do the things which the Lord hath commanded, for I know that the Lord giveth no commandments unto the children of men, save he shall prepare a way for them that they may accomplish the thing which he commandeth them" (1 Nephi 3:7).

God has not asked you to do anything that you aren't capable of doing—birth included. It is a commandment to multiply and replenish the earth, and God has given you the tools you need to do that. He knew it would be hard. But He is there, ready to magnify you.

MAGNIFICATION FROM YOUR GOD-GIVEN INSTINCTS

I remember the first birth I ever witnessed. I was in Alberta, Canada, at Glacier National Park. I was seventeen years old, and I saw a deer give birth to twins. I was sitting on a bench with my own twin sister, chatting and watching the sunset. A deer close by caught our attention, and at first we didn't even realize we were witnessing the miracle of birth. The mother deer did not seemed distressed at all. She made no sound and hardly moved. Moments later her first fawn arrived, and the second came quickly after. Several minutes later, they walked away with their mother. I didn't know what to think. It all just seemed so easy. Could I have really just seen a birth?

Obviously birth is much different for people. Human mothers tend to work quite a bit harder to deliver their young, and human babies are much more helpless. These are all good things because they ensure a stronger bond for humans than for animals. Unlike humans, who can gain knowledge and practice birthing techniques, animals only have their instincts to guide their births. When I think about Eve and what her births would have been like, she would have had to rely solely on her "animal" or maternal instincts. She had to listen to her body and do what came naturally. We don't know specifics, but it seems unlikely she had anyone to assist her, not a mother of her own and certainly not a midwife or a doctor. Her experience proves that we already have all the tools we need to give birth. And she did it! So can you.

Instincts guide women through births. Every woman in the scriptures gave birth without medical intervention. Most likely, they instinctually birthed in ways we still see women birthing in underdeveloped countries. Positions like squatting, kneeling, hands and knees, clinging to a tree or rope, standing on birth bricks, or sitting in an elevated birthing chair are typical delivery positions.[3] These upright positions assist the woman by adding the force of gravity. Positions like these also open the pelvis wider and put equal amounts of pressure on all sides of the perineum. Initially these women didn't know the significance of all they were doing. They were utilizing their birthing instincts. In reality, when left alone, birth is an involuntary event that can succeed all on its own.

I remember a particular client of mine who was so instinctual. I could tell that she wasn't worried about how she looked, sounded, or acted (which is rare for American women—we are so self-conscious). She let her labor lead the way. When she felt like she needed to move, she would move. She vocalized, she swayed. She labored so beautifully. In order to do this, a mother must feel safe and supported. She must also trust her body and tune into herself while she tunes out the rest of the world. I have often experienced women fighting their natural instincts while they labor. It is too embarrassing, and can sometimes make a woman feel too self-conscious and vulnerable to surrender to. This is not helpful. The more a woman can tune into herself and her instincts, the better she will be able to cope with her labor. But if she is worried about how she looks, what people will think of her, or how she is acting, she will be a hindrance to herself.

Much of what we do is instinctual. We rest when we are tired. We eat when we are hungry. We cry when we are sad and smile when we feel joy. Birthing instincts are harder to find because we need them so rarely throughout our lives and because we are fearful. Removing fear from your birth is the number one way to find your instincts. Replace your fear with faith and knowledge. While it is difficult—if not impossible—to remove all anxiety, if you focus on the normalcy of birth, you will be able to navigate your way through it safely and instinctually.

MAGNIFICATION FROM YOUR SUPPORT TEAM AND FROM PREPARATION

A woman can receive support during her birth in many ways: her mother, a friend, a skilled and compassionate nurse, and, of course, her husband. You do not have to be a doula to know how to support and nurture someone. What is most important is that the mother feels safe and supported, no matter who the support person is. Some women feel safer and more supported when they hire a doula because doulas are trained in how to support a laboring woman. Studies show that having a doula at a birth decreases the rates of Pitocin use, pain medications, and cesareans. Research also shows that women who have doulas present at their births are more likely to view their birth as a positive experience.[4]

As a doula, my role is to magnify my clients' ability to birth by providing physical, emotional, and informational support. Typically I offer all three types of support during each birth I attend, but the amount of each will vary depending on the client and on the birth. Initially, everyone is interested in physical support because women tend to worry the most about coping with the pain of contractions.

A woman can do dozens of things to lower her perception of pain during childbirth. The most successful strategies always involve relaxation and deep breathing. The ability to relax during contractions is key to all birthing methods, whether you choose the Lamaze, hypnobirthing, Bradley, or music birth methods. The physical support I provide aims at helping a woman relax and gives her a positive sensation to focus on.

Pleasure travels quickly to our brains. It is almost instantaneous. Pain travels slowly. There is a short delay between the cause of the pain and our brain realizing the presence of pain. Our brains can process a limited amount of information at any given time. When lowering our perception of pain in childbirth, the goal is to flood our brains with positive stimuli in order to block some of the negative stimuli. This is much more successful when a laboring mom is relaxed and actively working to focus on the comfort instead of the pain.

Between contractions I encourage my client to continue to breathe deeply and focus on the relief she is feeling. Unless the baby is positioned poorly in the pelvis, she should experience no pain when contractions aren't present. These breaks are longer than contractions, and a typical labor will have much more time without pain than time with it. A woman who can focus on how good it feels to have a short respite from contractions will cope much better than the woman who spends her break dreading the next contraction and bracing for it. This not only puts all of her concentration on her pain, but it also prevents relaxation.

When a new contraction starts, I encourage her to take a deep, cleansing breath. This ensures the oxygenation of the uterus and helps her relax. I then provide some sort of physical support, typically through massage. Most women respond well to lower back massage, neck massage, hand massage, and even foot massage if they find lying down to be comfortable. Sitting in a Jacuzzi tub, walking, and swaying on the birth ball are also successful comfort measures. The type of comfort measure I suggest will depend on how well the mother is coping and how the labor is progressing. If her labor is progressing slowly, I am more likely to recommend that she walk or move. If labor is progressing quickly, she may benefit more from focused relaxation.

During contractions I also provide emotional support by reminding the mom that she is doing a great job. Coping with contractions can be quite the mental exercise. No matter how well my client appears to be coping with her labor, I know that she is also wondering how much longer labor will last, if she will be able to make it that long, and if she will ask for pain medications. Laboring moms need constant encouragement, and they need to know that the people around them believe in their ability to give birth.

I often hear laboring moms say, "I don't know if I can really do this." I always point out that not only *can* she do this—she *is* doing it! Each contraction is purposeful and gets the mom closer to holding her baby.

Husbands are an extremely important part of offering physical and emotional support. While they can't take away the burden, they can ease it with their love and encouragement. In order for a husband to know how to support his wife physically and emotionally, he must become educated. Taking a childbirth education class is a great way for a couple to prepare together for their birth. Many of my clients express that their class helped them bond with their baby, and to each other. Find more information about how a husband can support his wife in chapter ten.

Whether my doula clients take a childbirth education class or not, I always meet with them prior to the birth to provide informational support. My goal is for all of my clients to go into their birth with a basic understanding of labor and delivery. I also want them to understand medical interventions and any associated risks and benefits. I teach and demonstrate a variety of comfort measures so they know what kinds of things we will be doing to cope with contractions. I also help them figure out what is most important to them for their particular birth.

The location of the birth and the progression of the birth determine what type of informational support I provide during the labor process. Women who deliver at home or at a birthing center typically receive more education from their midwives prior to the birth and will not have as many questions for me during their labor, nor will they have as many options since many interventions are not offered at these locations. Couples who birth at a hospital will have many more options, which leads to asking for much more information.

My job is not to tell a couple which decision to make. I offer unbiased, evidence-based information. My clients are free to choose for themselves what type of birth they desire, and I have seen a wide variety of births. Their choices will determine what future information they need from me.

A common question I get from my clients is, "Is this normal?" It is difficult for couples to decipher if what they are experiencing is normal, especially if they are having their first child. The realm of normal in childbirth is quite large, and knowing that everything is okay and "normal" regarding their birth can help a couple feel relaxed and confident.

Having the constant presence of a trusted resource can also help a couple maintain relaxation. Unlike a nurse or a doctor, doulas do not go home when their shift is over. A doula provides continuous labor support until the birth has occurred and medical assessments have proven that both mom and baby are doing well. Doula support typically spans the third trimester of pregnancy to several weeks after the birth. (See Appendix F for more information on doulas.)

MEDICAL MAGNIFICATION

Though studies show that mothers and babies do best when medical intervention is avoided whenever possible, at times it is needed and beneficial. Requiring medical magnification is not a sign of weakness or unrighteousness. The divine design of childbirth is perfect, but our bodies are not. When we have leaned on our Heavenly Father, utilized our instincts and education, and tried our best to achieve a natural birth—but still cannot achieve it—then we need intervention. In these circumstances, medical intervention is also a gift from a loving Heavenly Father.

It is imperative for all women desiring natural birth to remember that only 5 to 10 percent of women are truly incapable of giving birth vaginally.[5] It is these women who benefit greatly from medical advancements. This also means that a small group of women will leave their births with feelings of disappointment. Because of this, it is crucial for all women preparing to give birth to have an understanding of when medical intervention is needed and when it is not.

NOTES

1. Jeffrey R. Holland, "Motherhood: An Eternal Partnership with God," lds.org.
2. Sarah Buckley, "The Hidden Risks of Epidurals," *Mothering*, no. 133, November–December 2005; Carol Sakala and Maureen P. Corry, *Evidence-*

Based Maternity Care: What It Is and What It Can Achieve (New York: Milbank Memorial Fund, 2008).

3. Judy DeLoache and Alma Gottlieb, *A World of Babies* (Cambridge: Cambridge University Press, 2000), 66, 129, 160, 179, and 209.

4. Penny Simkin, "Position Paper: The Birth Doula's Contribution to Modern Maternity Care," *DONA International*, 2012.

5. Luz Gibbons et al., "The Global Numbers and Costs of Additionally Needed and Unnecessary Caesarean Sections Performed per Year: Overuse as a Barrier to Universal Coverage," *World Health Organization*, World Health Report: Background Paper, no. 30, (2010).

Section One

WORKSHEET

What surprised you the most about this section?

Were any of the concepts regarding natural childbirth difficult for you to accept? Why do you think that was?

How do you view birth differently after reading this section?

What hasn't changed about how you view birth?

Which type of magnification do you feel will be most valuable for your birth?

Section Two

THE MEDICALIZATION
OF A MIRACLE

Section two is written to help you understand the benefits and risks of common birth interventions. Many people are surprised to find out that most of what is done to improve birth is medically optional as opposed to medically necessary. Remember—giving birth is a normal, healthy aspect of being a female. As long as there are no medical conditions happening during a pregnancy (such as high blood pressure, gestational diabetes, and preeclampsia), there is nothing medical about it. When pregnancy and birth are progressing normally, all medical support is optional.

Medical intervention is necessary in childbirth when some type of pathology (something abnormal, unhealthy, or unsafe) accompanies the pregnancy or birth. During the next two chapters, we will discuss scenarios that warrant intervention and scenarios that don't. At times, the use of an intervention isn't medically warranted, but a woman still chooses it. Understanding the benefits and risks associated with birth interventions will help you determine what type of birth you desire and help you make decisions that will lead to the best outcome for your particular birth.

Chapter 4

HOW INDUCTIONS AND EPIDURALS CHANGE BIRTH

When Heavenly Father designed the female body, He configured a way for that body to create, protect, and give life. Natural childbirth versus medical childbirth debates did not exist. There was only childbirth. God *had* to design it in a way that would succeed. The human race was dependent on that. Obviously, we know that not every woman and child has survived childbirth. Because of this, science has looked for answers and ways to improve outcomes.

The medical world has certainly brought about advancements that save lives every day. Infants born early are now often given a second chance at life as they continue to grow and develop in the NICU under intense medical care and advancements. Women whose bodies could not achieve a vaginal birth are given the chance to bear children through cesarean birth. These are modern-day miracles, and I know many whose lives have been extremely blessed because of them. When intervention *is* needed, it does make birth safer. But all medical interventions carry potential risks.

As doctors strive to improve high-risk births, many low-risk births suffer. Over time, the majority of American births have incorporated some aspect of high-risk support, which opens up potential risks that do not need to be present in a low-risk setting. While the initial goal was to improve the outcomes of high-risk situations, we have done the exact opposite in low-risk settings; we have taken what wasn't working and have found ways to make it work, but we have also taken what *was* working and have made it less successful.

Somehow American birth has blurred the lines between high-risk and low-risk birth. Natural childbirth is scarce, and the use of midwives is minimal. This change in paradigm began in the late eighteen hundreds when the medical field was growing and starting to incorporate childbirth into its practices.

Wanting to be the sole care providers to pregnant women, doctors began running campaigns against midwives, saying they used old and dirty customs from the countries from which they immigrated. This appealed to the modern, industrialized American female. Giving birth in a hospital under the direction of a doctor was deemed superior to the time-proven success of home birth with a midwife. Later, feminists joined in the fight, saying that women shouldn't have to be subjected to the horrible pain and fatigue of childbirth. Pain medications released women of the "curse" of childbirth.[1]

In hindsight we know that many of the early interventions involved in birth were dangerous and that doctors did not understand the transfer of germs and disease. The early days of obstetrics brought about much risk, and even death, as puerperal fever quickly spread through maternity wards.

Heavenly Father has always been aware of the needs of the birthing woman and has continually done His part to protect birth. He cares so deeply about birth that being a midwife used to be a calling, and midwives were once set apart and ordained. Birth was viewed as a sacred event that LDS midwives were given the authority to administer blessings of strength to the laboring woman.[2] (During this time fathers were traditionally not present when their children were born.)

As the popularity of medical birth grew, Joseph Smith counseled midwives to follow the principles of the Word of Wisdom, and Brigham Young even discouraged the use of doctors during childbirth.[3] While the scientific reasoning behind their advice was unknown at the time, the prophets were inspired to give counsel that would protect the Saints during the early days of maternal medicine.

But just as most women did, LDS women began choosing doctors over midwives. Along with this choice came the high use of interventions as doctors experimented in new ways to improve childbirth and relieve the pain it caused. Recently, birth has become even more medicalized as the cesarean rate reaches new highs each year.[4]

The appropriate use of interventions magnifies birth, while the over-use of interventions can harm birth. Current studies show that birth interventions are grossly overused in America. The routine use of intervention has contributed to America having the highest rate of maternal mortality in the industrialized world, and one of the highest infant mortality rates.[5] In 1987, 6.6 women out of 100,000 died from giving birth.[6] By 2014 we had almost quintupled that number to 28 per 100,000 births![7] That puts the United States in sixtieth place for maternal mortality, meaning it is safer to give birth in fifty-nine other countries. The United States has also seen a 75 percent increase in severe morbidity and near-miss mortalities from 1998 to 2009.[8] These statistics are alarming because many women I speak with are under the assumption that giving birth is safer now than it used to be.

American families also have the highest costs associated with giving birth.[9] With the highest cost, wouldn't you expect the highest quality of care and the lowest mortality rate?

A March 2014 publication from the American College of Obstetrics and Gynecology (a leader in research and advocacy for childbirth and other women's health issues) points out that most pregnancies are low-risk, and encourages care providers to lower their cesarean rates as mortality and morbidity rates have increased along with cesarean rates.[10]

In January 2015, ACOG said that low-risk patients should be treated low-risk, and encouraged the use of midwives in freestanding birth centers to not only improve outcomes but to also lower the extreme cost of giving birth in the United States. They believe that by treating low-risk and high-risk patients differently, mortality and morbidity rates will decrease. They explain that the main causes of increased mortality and morbidity are obesity, diabetes, hypertensive disorders, and the increase of cesareans.[11]

You will learn in the next two chapters that several factors have contributed to the rising cesarean rate: the use of medical interventions during birth without medical need, a doctor's practice style, and women consenting to and even electing unnecessary cesareans.

Birth interventions were originally designed to assist births that could not be successful on their own, and there was a time when interventions were only used when truly needed. As time has passed, we have allowed many interventions to become a choice based on preference and even convenience. While we are now able to choose an optional intervention, we are never able to determine the consequence of that choice. And because all interventions carry potential risks, the only way to keep childbirth safe is to learn how to decipher when the benefits outweigh the risks.

INDUCTION

Inductions are an artificial way of starting labor. While there are several ways to induce labor, this chapter will focus on only two methods: sweeping (or stripping) the membranes and Pitocin induction. Sweeping the membranes is the process of a care provider using his/her fingers to separate the amniotic sac from the woman's uterus. This can sometimes stir up enough hormones for labor to physiologically begin on its own. In order for a care provider to attempt this, a woman must already be somewhat dilated. Pitocin induction occurs when artificial oxytocin is released into the woman's bloodstream through an IV. Pitocin does not physiologically start labor like sweeping the membranes does, but it typically does force the uterus to have contractions and creates a physical labor and birth in about two-thirds of the women who are induced this way.

Over time, doctors have been able to determine certain scenarios where moms or babies will be healthier if childbirth happens sooner than it would occur on its own. Should a woman or child's health be in jeopardy by continuing on with the pregnancy, induction is a fairly successful way to initiate labor so health concerns can be quickly treated or resolved.

Women experiencing high blood pressure, diabetes, cancer, or kidney disease can all benefit from inductions. If there is true evidence that the baby is not growing or thriving inside the womb (often due to problems with the placenta), an induction is also necessary.

In high-risk settings, inductions improve birth outcomes and give many women the opportunity to try for a vaginal birth. Without inductions, the only option for these cases would be cesarean. But in low-risk settings, inductions invite many potential physical and physiological risk factors into a birth that should have very low risk.

When my first child was just seven months old, my husband and I discovered we were already expecting another child. We were surprised but very happy because we had always hoped to have at least two children. My pregnancy had the typical hardships of fatigue and nausea. On their own, those trials are enough for any woman to dislike pregnancy. But those were the least of my worries. Three months into my pregnancy, my father passed away from cancer. Seven months in, my firstborn was diagnosed with a brain tumor. My personal life was falling part, and stress began to take a huge toll on me.

At thirty-four weeks, my cervix was already dilated to four centimeters, and I was placed on bed rest for several weeks. While the end of my pregnancy drew closer, so did my husband's graduation date and our corresponding moving date to Boise, Idaho, where he would begin his career. Because I was on bed rest and also taking care of my daughter as she recovered from brain surgery, I was doing very little to prepare for our move.

I expressed to my care provider the stress of not having enough time to pack our boxes before our move because it was difficult work to do with a large abdomen and zero energy. She asked if I would like her to strip my membranes. This appeared to be a wonderful idea, so I agreed to it without asking any follow-up questions and without truly understanding the risks of inducing a labor. I assumed that because we were inducing labor in a natural, hormonal way that it would be safe.

Honestly, the birth itself was safe. My labor progressed timely and did not require any medical support. At that point in my life, I didn't understand that a perfect labor didn't guarantee perfect health for myself and my newborn. Not once did I consider my child's readiness to be born, nor was I given any information regarding this.

Arriving two weeks before her due date, my little one was born barely over six pounds. She was beautiful and perfect, and considered healthy and full term. But she choked. A lot. It was terrifying. She would be nursing and then just stop breathing. I couldn't relax. I didn't dare. I was sure I wouldn't notice her choking and she would die in my arms without me even knowing. I couldn't sleep. I was so worried about her. My anxiety took over, and I experienced one of the hardest years of my life. I know that year would have been difficult no matter what. I had a lot on my plate for a young mom. But I have always felt that another week or two in the womb would have made a difference in my daughter's ability to nurse and breathe rhythmically (a common concern in infants born prematurely). I forced her to be born on a day that was convenient for me, and that was not fair to her. We both paid the price.

Almost ten years after her birth, in June 2015, researchers discovered that a fetus secretes surfactant—a chemical in the lungs essential for breathing—into the mother's uterus. This creates an inflammatory response in the mother's womb that helps initiate labor. This is the baby's way of saying "I'm ready." When we jumpstart labor before getting this crucial signal from our children, many of them are born with breathing difficulties.[12] Had I understood this, I never would have induced labor.

When considering induction, parents must understand the risks for both the mother and for the child. Studies show that babies who are born due to inductions are more likely to be premature, meaning they show signs of being born too soon, even if they are considered full term.[13] (See Appendix A to learn more about due dates and what it means to be full term.) Premature birth carries great risk factors: intellectual disabilities, breathing difficulties, hearing and vision loss, jaundice, feeding and digestive problems, and even death.[14]

Despite these frightening statistics, induction rates continue to increase. Not only does induction increase an infant's risk of a premature delivery, but it also invites many risks into the labor and birth.

Mothers who are induced begin their labors without the aid of pain-fighting endorphins. This makes inductions much more painful than naturally occurring labors. When oxytocin is given to a woman in the synthetic form of Pitocin, her uterus will probably respond by contracting. But because her brain is not producing the oxytocin, it doesn't know that it needs to make endorphins. The brain doesn't even know that her body is acting like it's in labor! These women are then less able to cope with the pain and rigor of contractions, leading to a desire to use pain medication. Because the brain is not controlling the labor, it is much less likely that the labor will progress normally.

When a woman is induced, medicine, instead of her brain, tells her body what to do. Her brain *should* tell her body what to do. It should create oxytocin and tell her uterus to contract. It should supply her with pain-fighting, energy-inducing endorphins. Depending on the point at which pharmaceutics are involved, the labor brain dials down, shuts off, or fails to start. When you separate your brain from your birth, you lose those valuable hormones and endorphins that fight pain, progress labor, and promote bonding.[15]

As a natural labor unfolds, one labor hormone leads to another. Oxytocin is the leader, and without it, the other hormones and chemicals needed for birth will not be produced. When we force a labor to start by tricking the body into thinking it has the right hormone, we rarely get a birth that progresses normally and requires no other intervention, and we always get a labor void of oxytocin and endorphins. Physiologically speaking, an induced labor is completely different from a labor that starts on its own. Most likely, the mother will not experience the after-birth high, and her brain will not be flooded with oxytocin or maternal instincts. This does not mean that she won't experience feelings of joy and love, but it does mean that she will not be experiencing the automatic flood of brain activity that occurs with a physiologic delivery.

Furthermore, Pitocin makes contractions last longer, which can lead to fetal distress, brain damage, and, in rare cases, even death.[16] Fetal distress is common during inductions, and I have seen it in at least half of the induced births I have attended. Fetal distress is one of the primary reasons that babies are born with the aid of forceps, vacuums, and cesareans.[17] Because fetal distress is often seen in births where Pitocin and pain medications are used, we can safely assume that fetal distress is also often avoidable and can result from a choice made earlier in the labor.

Receiving Pitocin (or any other optional intervention) does not guarantee an unwanted outcome. I have seen inductions go quickly and safely, but I have also seen inductions end in cesarean after an entire day or two of contractions that never led to cervical dilation. However, all of my clients whose labors eventually required a cesarean had received Pitocin earlier during their labors.

Studies show anywhere from 17 to 36 percent of first-time moms who are induced will receive cesareans,[18] even though leading health experts agree the cesarean rate should be between 5 and 10 percent.[19] A current Swedish study showed that induction more than triples a first-time mom's risk of needing an emergency cesarean, and almost doubles the risk of emergency cesarean for women who have already had a vaginal birth.[20]

Keep in mind that when we force a labor to start, the body and baby are often not ready for labor. The odds of a successful vaginal birth with a cervix that is not showing any signs of being ready for birth (like softness and moving forward) are low.[21]

In 2010 one of the major hospitals in Boise, Idaho, decided to take a stand against their high cesarean rates. Hospital administrators made one change: women could no longer be induced before thirty-nine weeks without true medical need. The cesarean rate drastically fell, proving that by choosing the day our child is born, we often choose to deliver them via cesarean. In one year, the cesarean rate for first-time moms considered to be low-risk plummeted from 18 percent to 4 percent![22]

In our busy society, it truly is an inconvenience to not know when your baby will be born. Most women do not enjoy living their life in limbo, wondering when labor will start. It is easy to see the appeal of elective induction. But in hindsight, many women who have chosen elective inductions did not find the painful contractions and longer labors to be appealing. While there are many instances where induction is prudent and scientifically backed, induction is a decision that shouldn't be taken lightly due to the many physical and physiological risks associated with it. While it can be difficult to wait for labor to begin on its own, it is still easier than a stressful birthing experience that could have been avoided.

Requiring induction can be difficult for a woman who has a strong desire to go into labor on her own and avoid interventions. That being said, women who legitimately require induction should feel no shame or remorse over receiving one. For example, women with dangerously high blood pressure have an increased risk of heart attack or stroke during their births. In this scenario, the risks of induction seem quite small compared to the risks the high blood pressure brings into the birth. But for a woman whose blood pressure is healthy, the added risk of induction is unnecessary.

Below is a chart with lists of proven and unproven reasons to consider induction. Women who find themselves in the left hand column

PROVEN REASONS TO CONSIDER INDUCTION	UNPROVEN REASONS TO BE INDUCED
Gestational diabetes	Past the due date (40 weeks)
Very high blood pressure	The doctor is about to leave town
Past 42 weeks	So baby can have a cool birthday
Health concern for mom that can't be resolved while she is still pregnant	Because mom and sister of pregnant woman reported needing to be induced
	Tired of waiting/impatience
	Because the doctor offers
	Fear of large baby

should prayerfully consider an induction, even if they had greatly hoped to avoid one. In these instances, the risk of remaining pregnant may be greater than the risks that accompany induction. Women in the right hand column should carefully decide if they are truly okay with the risks of induction, considering there is no medical need for one.[23]

Several years ago, I supported a woman through her fourth delivery, which was also her first natural birth. With the news of her fifth pregnancy, we both assumed that her birth would be similar to the one prior, and we both planned on another natural birth. But as mentioned before, it is key to always remain flexible. She explains:

> Delivering my fourth child without any interventions was a wonderful experience that I will always remember. I regard it as a very sacred experience where I got a tiny glimpse of what our Savior did for us in Gethsemane. It made me feel strong and so happy. I now know I can do hard things.
>
> So when I was expecting my fifth child I knew I wanted another natural birth. But at my thirty-seven-week check-up I was diagnosed with low amniotic fluid. I was told I would be monitored and tested every other day to determine if it was safe for me to wait until I went into labor on my own, or if I required an induction.
>
> I was fervently praying that my baby would be safe, and that I would be able to go into labor on my own. This is a good time for us all to remember that every one of our prayers are answered; it's just sometimes the answer is "no."
>
> On the fourth day my doctor determined it was no longer safe to wait, and my induction was scheduled for the next day. The morning I went in to have my baby I was still hopeful that despite being induced, I would still be able to deliver my baby without an epidural. With the help of my husband and doula, I handled the contractions tolerably well for quite some time.
>
> As my contractions became more unnaturally painful, I remember grasping on to my IV stand and noticed that the monitor on the front was flashing the word "oxytocin." I was completely distracted and flabbergasted! I don't know who they think they're fooling but let me tell you the truth! Oxytocin is natural and perfectly designed to cause contractions. Pitocin is man-made and NOT at all comparable to the real thing!

Around ten hours into my labor I was longing for my fourth delivery. Those contractions seemed like a gentle breeze compared to what my medically induced ones had become. Marie told me later that there was a point at the peak of each contraction where she could see my entire body uncontrollably shaking from the pain.

After over eleven hours of contractions my nurse checked me and I was still at a four centimeters. I looked over at my husband and had to concede that I had done all I could. At that point I was extremely grateful that epidurals exist. Because I could no longer feel the pain of the contractions, my doctor was able to turn up the Pitocin to speed up my slow progress. Cooper was born less than two hours later!

It truly is a miracle that no matter how they get here, the moment your precious baby gets placed in your arms everything is forgotten and all there is left is pure joy.[24]

EPIDURAL ANESTHESIA

It's no secret that labor is hard and that contractions are painful. Because of this, doctors and anesthesiologists have worked for decades for ways to medically relieve the pain of childbirth. Modern-day epidurals do just that. Epidurals effectively remove pain for 85 to 90 percent of the women who use them. Because of their high success rate, approximately 85 percent of women will choose epidural pain management during the births of their children. For many women, relieving pain during childbirth will help them feel relaxed and more confident in their ability to give birth.

One woman explains her reason for choosing an epidural like this: "For me the epidural was the way to go. I experienced a natural birth as well as three births with an epidural. I am glad that I can say I experienced both. However, for me, I felt more in control when I was free from pain and could focus on the overall situation rather than the pain in that moment."[25]

Epidurals can be especially beneficial to women who are afraid to experience the discomfort of childbirth. For some, experiencing a painful birth will make their birth a negative experience. I have had several clients who had positive birthing experiences *because* of their epidurals since their fear of the pain was all-encompassing and overshadowed the benefits that accompany a natural birth. Other women choose epidurals because they do not have anyone to support them through a natural birth, and the thought of achieving it alone is too overwhelming.

Epidurals give moms (and dads) a chance to rest and even sleep during their labors. This can be particularly helpful for labors that have progressed slowly, been extraordinarily long or tiring, or occurred in the night or when the mother is already experiencing much fatigue. Epidurals also aid in inductions, as Pitocin often leads to painful and long labors.

For many, the decision to choose an epidural will seem somewhat minor, but it is actually the most influential decision a woman will make during her labor because of the likelihood of that choice determining how the rest of the birth progresses.

It is helpful to understand that electing an epidural is a choice that cannot be taken back, and the side effects cannot be removed once they are present. In the long run, an epidural can actually take away freedom of choice because many choices will no longer be available due to the confines of the epidural. Almost all natural methods of supporting and augmenting a labor become impossible because they require the mother to be able to get out of the bed. Should contractions slow down, as they typically do in a medicated birth, the woman can no longer choose to walk or change positions to encourage them to start up again. The only option is Pitocin. Being restricted to the bed and continually monitored takes away the majority of the options a woman could have at her disposal during her labor.

Understanding where your choices can take you as your birth progresses is critical. I recommend always trying to look ahead one or two steps to ensure that the current decision will not negatively affect the future of your birth. For some women, losing the ability to utilize natural methods will not be bothersome, and the decision to receive an epidural will be an easy one. To others, losing the option of natural methods will be extremely frustrating and possibly disappointing.

While many women tell me they desire an epidural, no one has ever told me they desire the use of Pitocin in their labor. Few understand that an epidural frequently leads to the use of Pitocin because the epidural physiologically disconnects the woman's brain from her labor, causing oxytocin production to decrease, which spaces out and weakens contractions. This lack of oxytocin almost triples the likelihood of a labor requiring Pitocin.[26] The combination of epidural drugs and Pitocin is much more difficult on the infant than the epidural alone,[27] which increases the likelihood of fetal distress.[28] And as we learned previously in the chapter, fetal distress often leads to forcep- and vacuum-assisted deliveries, as well as cesareans.

Once a woman is finally dilated to ten centimeters, she still has many obstacles to overcome. Due to her epidural, she cannot feel the natural urge to push, which makes pushing more difficult, tiring, and scary. Because mothers with epidurals are unable to bear weight and change position, they have to deliver their baby while laying on their backs: the hardest and least efficient way to deliver a child.[29]

Babies are four times more likely to be posterior (facing the wrong way in the pelvis, which often causes much discomfort and slows labor progress) when a woman labors with an epidural.[30] The overwhelming majority of labors with an epidural and a posterior baby (up to 74 percent of first-time moms) will require an instrumental delivery with forceps or a vacuum, or a cesarean.[31]

Epidurals also lengthen labor. This may seem minor when the woman is not experiencing any prolonged pain, but it does put extra stress on the baby and will put much more pressure on the woman's pelvic floor muscles while she pushes. Prolonged pushing is not only exhausting, but it also increases instances of hemorrhoids and vaginal injury. These issues can often be long-term as opposed to the short-term discomfort experienced in birth.

A woman without an epidural has much more freedom, as well as the other noted benefits of laboring naturally. She is free to move and try different positions. She also can feel the urge to push and use her natural instincts to guide her labor. This puts less pressure on her perineum, makes her less likely to have vaginal injury, and speeds up her post-birth recovery. It also speeds up the process of delivering her child.

Women who deliver without epidurals also report higher levels of satisfaction with their birth.[32] Conversely, women who report the highest amounts of pain relief report the lowest levels of birth satisfaction.[33] I suspect the reason for this is that most women who choose to receive an epidural do not understand the ramifications of that choice and are often upset when their epidural causes them to experience the things they most wanted to avoid. Does this mean that every woman with an epidural is unsatisfied with her birthing experience? Of course not. But it does point out that removing the pain of childbirth does not guarantee feeling good about how your birth went. It suggests that many factors contribute to birth satisfaction and that relieving pain isn't as great a factor as one may suspect.

There is no research showing that an epidural makes labor or vaginal birth safer. While it does tend to relax the mom and satisfy her desire for pain management, it makes her susceptible to many risks. Physiological risks include the lack of oxytocin and endorphins. This can impede labor progress and prevents the birth high, heightened bonding, and heightened maternal instincts that oxytocin and endorphins provide. Associated physical risks range from minor to life threatening and include dangerous drop in blood pressure (approximately 50 percent), maternal fever, spinal headaches (1 percent), long-term nerve damage, muscle weakness, postpartum hemorrhage (doubles risk), and vaginal injury. One out of every four thousand women will experience life-threatening reactions to their epidural due to cardiac arrest, respiratory arrest, or an epidural abscess.[34]

At first glance, statistics like 1 percent and one out of four thousand seem quite minor. But when you consider how many women give birth each year, these statistics affect thousands of women. Approximately four million babies are born each year in the United States, and more than three million of them will have mothers with epidurals. Thus, more than thirty thousand new moms will experience a debilitating spinal headache that can last for six weeks, and almost a hundred of them will come close to death.

When deciding if you desire an epidural, it is important to remember that the discomfort of labor is not a risk. Experiencing the pain of contractions actually makes your birth safer. However, for many women, the pain involved is a definite con. For this reason, I encourage women to weigh the benefits and risks, not the pros and cons. Natural birth certainly has many cons. It can be intimidating, tiring, and painful, but none of those items invite risk into the birth. Science clearly shows us that natural birth has the lowest amount of risk, even though it has some undesirable cons. (Don't you just love opposition in all things?)

EFFECTS ON BREASTFEEDING

At birth, a mother's breasts will already have colostrum (a low-volume type of milk that is full of fat and antibodies). Within several days, colostrum should be replaced with breast milk. Once the baby is born and the placenta is delivered, the pregnancy hormones, progesterone and estrogen, rapidly decrease, communicating that it is now time to produce milk instead of supporting a pregnancy. Similar to labor, lactogenesis (the process of the woman's milk coming in) is dependent on physiological triggers. The first trigger is the drop in progesterone and estrogen. The second trigger is an increase of oxytocin and prolactin, which is caused by the baby suckling. When a baby suckles the breast, prolactin and oxytocin are released and communicate to the mother's body that milk needs to be produced.

A thriving newborn will initiate breastfeeding shortly after birth. During the first hour or two directly after birth, newborn reflexes are heightened. This is designed to help them survive. Their sucking reflex is strong, and it is important for infants to nurse as soon as possible after they are born to imprint the form of nursing with a correct latch onto their brains. The period of heightened nursing reflexes ensures that a baby can survive outside the womb and also ensures breast milk production. After this hour or two, babies become very tired and will sleep for several hours. If the opportunity to nurse is missed, five or six hours may pass before the child is awake enough to nurse. By then they are incredibly hungry, often fussy, and their sucking reflex is not on overdrive as it was intended to be during their initial feeding.

Unfortunately, science shows us that the medicine in epidurals quickly passes the placenta[35] and lowers nursing reflexes and instincts in the newborn.[36]

When a newborn's reflexes are dulled due to medicinal interventions, they are born sleepy and miss out on the blessings of the heightened reflex period, just as a woman misses out on her period of heightened oxytocin. Medical birth impedes both the mother's and the infant's ability to breastfeed because it lowers maternal instincts and hormones and dulls the infant's reflexes. Dulled newborn reflexes contribute to delayed lactogenesis because the mother's breasts are not getting the signals they need from the baby to produce milk. This not only delays the mother's milk coming in, but it can also contribute to low milk supply and prevents breastfeeding success in many women. For the infant it can lead to poor weight gain and even failure to thrive.

Studies also show that it takes more than four times as long for an infant's liver to process the toxins it receives from birth medications[37] but nurses and doctors have told me that they feel some infants take much longer. An experienced NICU nurse shared with me that she often sees infants with effects of toxicity for thirty-six to forty-eight hours after birth. This is a lot of work for a tiny liver that has never had to process toxins before. This makes babies tired, irritable, and neurologically less able to breastfeed.[38] A baby that isn't nursing is getting hungrier, fussier, and more difficult to soothe. With about 85 percent of women receiving pain medication, you can easily see why so many of them are not having success with breastfeeding.

But it's not just pain medications that are impeding breastfeeding. IV fluids can also make breastfeeding more difficult because they cause the breasts and areolas to swell, causing extra discomfort during the early days of nursing. Studies show that women who receive IV fluids during birth are more likely to wean early on.[39]

Breastfeeding provides optimal nutrition and ensures that a child's needs of being held and comforted are met. It keeps oxytocin levels high and bonding ongoing. Breast milk is full of antibodies and is the number-one way to protect your child from illness. When a mother kisses her child, the pathogens found on the child's skin will affect the woman's breast milk, and antibodies will be created specifically for the pathogens found.[40] This not only helps babies stay healthy, but also it is proof of God's love and concern for His children. Like childbirth, breastfeeding was designed to not only give and sustain life, but to provide optimal health and bonded relationships.

While formula can be a true lifesaver in certain scenarios, it is important to understand that formula-fed babies get sick more often and to a worse degree. A 2010 cost analysis shows that the United States incurs at least thirteen billion dollars per year in excess costs due to pediatric illness because of low breastfeeding rates.[41] Formula is harder for a baby to digest, is expensive, does not provide the natural immunity breast milk provides, and often separates mom and baby.

If breastfeeding is important to you, it is helpful to know that almost all women are capable of breastfeeding. Some women will need very little support, and others will need a great deal of support. Should your baby struggle with nursing initially, it is important to maintain close contact (preferably skin to skin) with your baby to encourage oxytocin production. You will also need to use a breast pump to ensure that your nipples are getting the stimulation they need to signal the production of prolactin and oxytocin. Even if breastfeeding is difficult during the first few weeks, with the right amount of education and support, almost all women will be able to nurse.

EPIDURAL ALTERNATIVES

Women desiring natural childbirth should approach their births expecting to experience a certain amount of discomfort. There is talk of pain-free births, but that is uncommon. (Our epidural rate is evidence enough that the overwhelming majority of women consider childbirth to be painful.) And even women who claim to have painless births still describe their births as intense or pressure-filled, and to other women those sensations will be viewed as pain. Whether you view it as pain or pressure, childbirth is difficult, and expecting it not to be will leave you ill-prepared for it. However, there is much you can do to lower your perception of pain. While expecting pain, you can also expect yourself to be capable of coping with the pain. You can trust that the pain will not be intolerable.

Nothing takes away pain as well as an epidural. So if avoiding pain is the number one goal of your birth, you will not be satisfied with the recommendations I offer below. But for women hoping for a natural birth or hoping to labor for as long as possible before getting an epidural, you will find these recommendations to be helpful. Keep in mind that the longer you go before receiving medications, the less time there is for anything to go wrong, and the more time you and your baby will benefit from the naturally occurring labor.

RELAXATION

A woman's ability to remain relaxed during her labor is key to lowering the perception of pain. I tell my clients that 70 percent of getting through a natural birth is relaxation. For most, mastering relaxation will require practice. Training the body to breathe deeply and release tension during every exhale is extremely helpful. The best way to learn relaxation techniques is to take a childbirth education class geared toward natural childbirth. Even if you do not intend to go for a natural delivery, these classes will be the most efficient at teaching relaxation and coping skills.

POSITIVE STIMULI

The remaining 30 percent of coping through contractions is a combination of outside stimuli that provide comfort, happiness, or distraction. This includes, but is not limited to massage, aromatherapy, music, art, positive affirmations, sitting in a large bath tub, hot/cold packs, affection, and even prayer.

Nitrous Oxide

Europe has administered nitrous oxide to laboring moms for decades, but it is only recently beginning to get attention in the United States. Nitrous oxide is commonly known as the "laughing gas" that dentists offer. Many women find that the nitrous takes just enough of the edge off to get them through their contractions. But as with any other medicine, there are benefits and risks.

One major benefit of nitrous is how safe it is. It leaves the mother's body so quickly that it never reaches her baby. When a woman receives Pitocin or an epidural, her baby must be monitored continually because of the risk of fetal distress. Because nitrous does not reach the baby, no extra monitoring is required. The mother administers the nitrous herself and can decide when she would like it and when she is fine without it. Should the woman not enjoy using it, she can quickly stop and return to feeling normal within seconds.

I have seen several women use nitrous at the end of their labors, and have seen it make a big difference in how they cope through transition. One thing to understand is that it will not take away the pain. It elevates the mood so the mother does not care about the pain as much. For women desiring a removal of pain, nitrous will be a big disappointment. From what I have witnessed, I feel that the women who benefit most from nitrous are the women who desire natural birth but find themselves really struggling near the end of their labor.

Currently nitrous is not offered in most hospitals, but its use is expanding. If this is something you would be interested in using during your delivery, make sure to tell your care provider. It is offered in the hospitals where I live because the care providers asked the hospitals to supply it.

Conclusion

Research shows that inductions and epidurals have not improved low-risk birth. Yet many women are completely unaware of this and make choices that they think have been proven to be safe. When considering medical interventions, it is of the utmost importance to understand the ramifications of choosing them. In doing so, birth outcomes can improve, and women can have greater birth satisfaction.

For a quick review of benefits and risks, see Appendix B.

NOTES

1. Abby Epstein, *The Business of Being Born*, 2008, film.
2. Jenne Erigero Alderks, "Rediscovering the Legacy of Mormon Midwives," *Sunstone* no. 166 (2012).
3. Ibid.
4. Carol Sakala and Maureen P. Corry, *Evidence-Based Maternity Care: What It Is and What It Can Achieve* (New York: Milbank Memorial Fund, 2008).
5. Francine Coeytaux, Debra Bingham, and Nan Strauss, "Maternal Mortality in the United States: A Human Rights Failure," *Contraception Editorial*, March 2011.
6. Ibid.
7. Ken Hanly, "The U.S. ranks 50th in maternal mortality globally," *Digital Journal*, March 9, 2014, http://www.digitaljournal.com/life/health/the-usa-ranks-50th-in-maternal-mortality-globally/article/375372#ixzz2w5jxQty0.
8. "Levels of Maternal Care, Obstetric Care Consensus" *ACOG*, February 2015.
9. Sakala and Corry, *Evidence-Based Maternity Care.*
10. "Safe Prevention of the Primary Cesarean Delivery," *ACOG*, March 2014.
11. Ibid.
12. "Molecular mechanisms within fetal lungs initiates labor," *ScienceDaily*, accessed June 22, 2015, http://www.sciencedaily.com/releases/2015/06/150622162023.htm.
13. Sakala and Corry, *Evidence-Based Maternity Care*; Debbie Amis, "Healthy Birth Practices: #1 Let Labor Begin on its Own," *Lamaze International*, 2003.
14. "National Prematurity Awareness Month," *CDC*, http://www.cdc.gov/features/prematurebirth/.
15. Amis, "Healthy Birth Practices"; Sakala and Corry, *Evidence-Based Maternity Care*; Sarah Buckley, "The Hidden Risks of Epidurals," *Mothering*, no. 133, November–December 2005.
16. "Frequently Asked Questions," *ACOG*, 2012, 154.
17. Sakala and Corry, *Evidence-Based Maternity Care*; Debbie Amis, "Healthy Birth Practices."
18. Christopher Glantz, "Term Labor Induction Compared with Expectant Management," *Obstetrics and Gynecology* 115, no. 1 (January 2010), 70–76.

19. Luz Gibbons et al., "The Global Numbers and Costs of Additionally Needed and Unnecessary Caesarean Sections Performed per Year: Overuse as a Barrier to Universal Coverage," *World Health Organization*, World Health Report: Background Paper, no. 30 (2010).

20. Malin Thorsell et al., "Induction of labor and the risk for emergency cesarean section in nulliparous and multiparous women," *Nordic Federation of Societies of Obstetrics and Gynecology*, 2011.

21. "Frequently Asked Questions," *ACOG*, 2012, 154.

22. Taught by the head nurse at the Idaho Perinatal Project Annual Conference, 2010.

23. Amis, "Healthy Birth Practices."

24. Personal correspondence with Emily Perry.

25. Personal correspondence with Aubrey Tueller.

26. Buckley, "The Hidden Risks of Epidurals."

27. Ibid.

28. Ibid; Henci Goer, *The Thinking Woman's Guide to a Better Birth* (New York: The Berkley Publishing Group 1999), 134.

29. Joyce DiFranco, "Healthy Birth Practices, #5 Avoid Giving Birth on the Back and Follow the Body's Urges to Push," *Lamaze International*, 2003.

30. Buckley, "The Hidden Risks of Epidurals."

31. Ibid.

32. Ibid.

33. Ibid.

34. Ibid.

35. Sema Kuguoglu et al., *Breastfeeding After a Cesarean Delivery*, ed. Dr. Raed Salim (2010), http://www.intechopen.com/books/cesarean-delivery/breastfeeding-after-a-cesarean-delivery.

36. William and Martha Sears, *The Birth Book*, (Massachusetts: Little, Brown and Company, 1994), 173–74; Buckley, *The Hidden Risks of Epidurals*; Sakala and Corry, *Evidence-Based Maternity Care*.

37. Buckley, *The Hidden Risks of Epidurals*.

38. Ibid.

39. Sonya Kujawa-Myles et al., "Maternal intravenous fluids and postpartum breast changes: a pilot observational study," *International Breastfeeding Journal*, 10, no. 18 (2015).

40. Kristen Tea, "10 Things You Might Not Know About Breastfeeding, *Mothering*, October 2015, http://www.mothering.com/articles/10-things-might-not-know-breastfeeding/.

41. Prevention and Public Health Funds for Breastfeeding Promotion Efforts, 2011; USBC Letter to Congress—$15M in Prevention and Public Health Funds for Breastfeeding Promotion Efforts, March 2011.

Chapter 5

THE TRUTH ABOUT CESAREANS

*M*ost of us know a woman who legitimately needed a cesarean. For many, surgical birth is a godsend. When used appropriately, cesareans make births possible that otherwise would have ended in death. However, research clearly shows that cesareans are used too liberally in the United States, and their overuse contributes to poor birth outcomes, as well as long-term ramifications for birthing women.

Currently, 33 percent of American women will give birth via cesarean, even though the World Health Organization (a forum of leading health experts from around the globe) believes that only 5 to 10 percent of births will actually *require* cesarean delivery. They also state, "There is no justification for any region to have a cesarean rate higher than 10 to 15 percent"[1] as multiple studies show an increase in rates of mortality and morbidity in mothers and infants when the cesarean rate increases.[2] With these statistics, we learn that *at least* 70 percent of women receiving cesareans do not truly need the procedure.

What long- and short-term effects does this place on American mothers? What are the risks for women and for infants? What has contributed to the high cesarean rates in America? What are the proven reasons for performing a cesarean? And are unproven reasons being utilized? What can be done to lower our numbers? It is important for patients and providers to understand the answers to these questions, as we all have the common goal of healthy birth outcomes.

RISKS[3]

Cesareans are major abdominal surgery. Based on the research, the benefits of one do not outweigh the risks unless there is medical proof that the baby cannot be born safely with a vaginal birth. Maternal risks include blood clots and stroke, surgical injury, problems with anesthesia, longer hospitalization (they are also more likely to require re-hospitalization), infection, poor birth experience, less contact with newborn, breast-feeding difficulties, intense pain that can lead to prolonged postpartum pain, poor overall mental health and self-esteem, poor overall functioning, emergency hysterectomy, and even maternal death.

In addition, many risks associated with cesareans may compromise a woman's ability to bear more children. These risks should be taken seriously by any woman hoping to have more children. They include involuntary infertility; reduced fertility due to decreased desire to have more children; ectopic pregnancy; placenta problems including placenta previa, placenta accrete, and placental abruption (all conditions that require subsequent cesareans); and uterine rupture. The risk of uterine rupture is low but would require an emergency cesarean.

Rates of severe morbidity (complications like hemorrhage that requires hysterectomy or blood transfusion, cardiac arrest, renal failure, blood clots—which often lead to stroke—and major infection) triple with a cesarean delivery compared to vaginal birth.[4] The more cesareans a woman has, the more she is at risk: the risk increases with each surgery.[5]

Increased risks for the infant also exist: initial breathing struggles, respiratory morbidity, asthma, allergies, premature birth, infection, and stillbirth. Vaginal birth, medicated or natural, provides unique benefits for the infant, which helps them thrive. Labor puts a healthy amount of stress on a fetus, which in turn helps the baby breathe at birth, assists in expelling amniotic fluid from the baby's lungs, increases blood flow and energy supply to the baby, increases immunity, and helps the baby exhibit behaviors that trigger bonding in the mother. Vaginal birth also exposes the infant to healthy bacteria from the mother's birth canal.[6] Many babies who do not experience the healthy stress of labor and exposure to bacteria will struggle.

Depending on insurance coverage, a cesarean birth could potentially cost much more financially. This is another long-term risk that can put a strain on families—especially families hoping for more children, trying to live on one income, and striving to be full tithe payers.

The decision to have a cesarean should not be taken lightly. Seeking a second opinion and fasting and praying about the matter are all helpful and appropriate responses should your provider recommend a cesarean.

What Contributes to High Cesarean Rates

The world of obstetrics is ever changing, as research eventually proves which methods are beneficial and which are not. In between the implementation of new interventions and the completion of research to determine their effectiveness and safety, there will always be women experiencing unknown side effects. During this time, care providers will form their own opinions on effectiveness and safety, and build their practicing style around those beliefs. Couples will put their trust in unproven methods, making these methods socially acceptable and approved of.

Current research shows that the drastic increase in cesareans has not improved birthing outcomes, like many assumed it would. Studies show that cesarean birth increases maternal morbidity and mortality in low-risk women.[7] These statistics are hard to believe since many couples are under the false impression that a cesarean birth is safer than it actually is. They assume that they have been offered a safe solution and are unaware that they can often refuse to consent to the procedure. Fear is also involved, because a mother will consent to anything if she feels that her child's well-being is compromised. Blindly agreeing to a potentially dangerous medical procedure has led to a social acceptance of the high cesarean rate and an over-medicalization of birth in general.

We have already discussed how changing God's design for birth through the use of inductions and epidurals has led to an increase in cesarean birth, but that is just one side of the equation. It isn't just the choices that women are making. Our high cesarean rates have much to do with the medical paradigm itself. I believe many factors have brought us to such a high cesarean rate: timeliness of incorporating change, variability within the medical field, medical educational focus on cesareans, cost of malpractice insurance and fear of lawsuits, and even compassion for the laboring woman whose labor is progressing slowly.

Timeliness of Incorporating Change

In 2008, two leading researchers and educators in the field of childbirth, Carol Sakala and Maureen P. Corry, did an extensive literature review of maternity care in America. After reviewing hundreds of studies, they were able to see a clear difference in what the scientific evidence proves to be safest for moms and babies and what is actually taking place in American births. Their paper, "Evidence-Based Maternity Care: What It Is and What It Can Achieve," clearly shows that natural birth is safest for women and their infants. It also notes that the routine use of interventions causes more harm than good, that the cesarean rate is much too high, and that birth outcomes in other countries are far better than the United States.[8]

Their research and current research from the American Congress of Obstetricians and Gynecologists strongly encourages the medical world to decrease the cesarean rate,[9] but change like this takes time. Practice styles, procedures, and habits cannot change overnight. Some providers already work diligently to keep rates low, but we also know that some providers have very high rates. Those with high rates will have to greatly adapt to meet desired statistics. This may require educational support, which would also add to the time frame.

Incorporating change and basing our birthing decisions on evidence takes time and effort from the medical field, as well as from expectant parents. Informed couples want to benefit from the proven, positive contributions from the medical field. They want to take prenatal care, blood screenings, ultrasounds, and even interventions when proven necessary, and combine them with the proven benefits of natural childbirth and decreased intervention rates. Educating the next generation of birthers also takes time, as does changing opinions that have been socially accepted for many years.

MEDICAL VARIABILITY

Studies show that there is much variability among practices and hospitals when it comes to cesarean rates. The decision to perform a cesarean is the judgment call of the provider. Depending on that provider's birth philosophy, training, and expertise, some will have acceptable cesarean rates, and some will not. Because many of the reasons cesareans are performed are not based on evidence, cesarean rates will vary greatly, with some states reporting a 20 percent cesarean rate while others are pushing 40 percent, and one hospital reporting 7.1 percent and another reporting 69.9 percent![10] The reason we have high cesarean rates isn't that all doctors overuse the procedure. It is because some of them do, and they overuse it greatly.

Among obstetricians, there is a wide variability of birth approaches and cesarean rates. I have witnessed this variability in practices many times over the last twelve years in my professional work. I have seen doctors who trust birth greatly. They offer their support but don't insist on it. Many encourage their patients to be patient and assure them that they are capable and strong.

I have also seen providers start pushing for interventions at the first sign of anything not going perfectly. I recently attended a birth of a woman who was delivering her third child. Her first two births went smoothly, and she delivered both of her children without intervention. Like her first two labors, she progressed quickly with number three and was almost ready to push when we arrived at the hospital.

Her baby's heart rate was not optimal. Between one hundred twenty and one hundred sixty is ideal, and doctors also like to see frequent changes in heart rate to show that the baby is tolerating the labor well. Her baby's rate was in the nineties during contractions and would slowly creep back up into the one hundred twenties once the contraction was over. Lowered heart rate is fairly common during pushing, so I was surprised and alarmed when the on-call doctor immediately pushed for a cesarean.

Her baby was posterior (meaning he was facing the wrong way in the pelvis), and while it is harder to deliver a baby positioned like this, it happens often. There was no reason to think that this woman couldn't deliver vaginally—she had already done so twice! This doctor's overreaction sent both of my clients into a tailspin of panic. Dad fainted, and Mom began crying and screaming. The environment was chaotic. I couldn't believe what was happening, especially since she had only pushed once or twice and the baby's heart rate was recovering.

Seconds later the doctor that my clients had hired arrived. She suggested we all take a deep breath and reassess. The labor nurse and I asked if the mother could try pushing in a different position. Because she was laboring naturally, we were able to get her into a hands-and-knees position, and the heart rate immediately stabilized. Within ten minutes, this mother delivered her child.

Had her chosen doctor not arrived in time, this woman would have had a cesarean. These two doctors viewed birth very differently. It's clear that in no way did this birth require intervention. Also notice that if she had opted for an epidural, she definitely would have had a cesarean because her ability to change positions made the difference for her child.

EDUCATIONAL FOCUS ON CESAREANS

My husband and I are part of a couples' book club. Each month we get together with several other couples for dinner and a literary/intellectual discussion. (Sometimes we even talk about the book we read!) It has turned out to be a dynamic group of Church members. All of the mothers are highly educated and have chosen to stay home and raise their children. All of the men are intelligent, working professionals. Among us there is an eccentric doula (that would be me), a nurse anesthetist, and a medical student. Over the years, this combination has provided amazing and insightful conversations, including discussions on natural and medical childbirth. Childbirth was a particularly popular topic during the time our medical student friend was doing his obstetrics rotation. Prior to my friendship with him, I had always been curious about what obstetricians know and think about natural childbirth.

I discovered that while my friend was *extremely* educated and understood the human body at a much higher level than I do, my understanding of the benefits of natural childbirth was greater than his. He explained that the focus of the training he received at his particular medical school was not focused on natural childbirth, why it is healthier and safer, or how to support it. Instead his education focused on how to medically manage a birth. Because almost 80 percent of birthing women choose epidurals and half of birthing women receive Pitocin,[11] it is prudent that medical training focus on this.

Due to the high use of interventions, it is rare for a resident doctor to have the opportunity to observe and support a natural birth during the final stages of their education.[12] This has serious ramifications because these are the future doctors that women will trust with their vaginal births. In addition, new doctors to the field report feeling less confident in delivering a baby with forceps or a vacuum as opposed to doing a cesarean.[13] This obviously contributes to the high cesarean rate. It was assumed that cesareans would decrease neonatal morbidity, but studies actually show there is no difference in neonatal morbidity when comparing an instrumental vaginal delivery to a cesarean.[14] Should these trends continue, vaginal birth with an epidural will become almost obsolete. If our providers do not feel competent supporting a difficult vaginal delivery and our mothers do not feel comfortable with natural childbirth, the cesarean rate will continue to skyrocket. An educational shift is needed to help new doctors feel competent in all areas regarding birth.

Obstetrical education does not appear to emphasize how to avoid cesareans, nor are doctors around much during the labor when the woman is making choices that would either increase or decrease her need for a cesarean. As we discussed in chapter one, a woman's lack of education regarding medical interventions also increases the national cesarean rate.

MALPRACTICE FEARS

Studies show that states with high costs of malpractice insurance have higher cesarean rates.[15] If providers are worried about a potential lawsuit, they may opt for a cesarean because it guarantees that providers can prove they did everything in their power to prevent a poor outcome. Perhaps our culture of fear forces doctors to overuse interventions. I have personally heard obstetricians refer to routine intervention as an insurance policy, almost as if they're saying, "Just in case something will go wrong, I will treat you like it already has." But with this mind-set, many women suffer the effects of unneeded intervention.

COMPASSION

Midwives and obstetricians have chosen their profession because they want to help women and children. When a woman is struggling with a difficult or abnormally long labor, it is human nature to want to relieve her of that struggle. Several of my clients have received cesareans that were not medically indicated. Instead, the care provider offered the procedure out of compassion for how difficult the birth appeared to be, saying something like, "I hate to see you like this," or "If you are ready to have your baby, I can give you a cesarean." These are altruist intentions but are often based in short-term thinking instead of a long-term perspective of how the cesarean may affect the woman in the future. When medical decisions are determined by emotions instead of evidence, the rates of evidence-based practicing goes down and the rates of unnecessary interventions goes up.

PROVEN AND UNPROVEN REASONS TO PERFORM A CESAREAN

The most thorough and up-to-date research found that the following were the top five reasons for performing cesareans:

1. Suspected macromasia (fear that the baby is too large to be born vaginally).

2. Multiple gestation (more than one baby).

3. Fetal malpresentation.

4. Fetal distress.

5. Labor dystocia (the failure of a labor to progress).[16]

SUSPECTED MACROMASIA: Cesarean for fear of a large baby has been largely discredited through scientific research,[17] though it is clearly still being used to justify a cesarean birth. There is no way to know beforehand how big a baby is, or to know if that baby will fit through the mother's pelvis.

I often have clients choose to induce labor after their provider has encouraged them to because they fear the baby is overly large. (Women in general seem to be nervous about giving birth to a large baby, even though large babies are born vaginally every day.) But research proves that estimates of fetal weight are imprecise and that high birth weight warranting a cesarean is rare.[18] Most of the time, the baby is smaller than the provider anticipated. I even had one client who received a cesarean for suspected macromasia only to deliver a baby who was slightly under seven pounds—a completely average, even trending toward small, baby. I have also seen small women deliver large babies naturally. There is no way to predict how large a baby is or how successful a vaginal birth can be.

MULTIPLE GESTATION: When a woman is carrying more than one child, it is somewhat common for one of the babies to not be in an optimal position for a vaginal birth. Not much can be done about this. From what I have seen in my geographical area, certain care providers are much more willing to support vaginal twin births and more experienced in doing so. Women expecting multiples will want to consider seeking out these types of care providers.

My twin sister and I were born via cesarean. Due to our positioning inside our mother's womb, it would have been life-threatening for all of us had a vaginal birth been attempted. Obviously, in a case like ours, a cesarean was the best option. As you will see below, it wasn't easy. Here is our birth story, in my mother's words:

From the beginning of my pregnancy, all of the doctors I met with explained to me that I might end up having a C-section because of having twins, and the possible complications that could present themselves. Honestly, I was nervous about going through labor because I was often in bed for three days during my periods, and no amount of medication ended that pain, so I was not against receiving a C-section. One doctor even suggested to me that I could deliver one baby vaginally and the other would possibly have to be C-section because of positioning. That to me was not an option! If it was to be a C-section because one child needed it, then it would be for both.

I went into labor around thirty-seven weeks. My water broke and immediately the pains were three to four minutes apart. At the hospital, the doctor wanted to do a quick x-ray to find out positioning of the babies because my labor was not progressing. Ten minutes later he was in the room showing me how baby number one was lying across the cervix, and there was no way out.

Things had to happen fast because of the stress on my body and the stress on the babies. Instead of having an epidural and being able to watch my babies be born, I had to be put under for an emergency C-section. During the surgery I had several complications due to high blood pressure, and I had a small stroke. Because of this, I spent a great amount of time in recovery. My twin girls were taken to the nursery during this time. My second born was having problems with her breathing and was on oxygen for twelve hours. Once I was stabilized, I was able to look through the nursery window. I was able to see my first-born, and then they laid her on my chest for just a of couple minutes. But I could not even see my second born because she was further away from the window due to her needing oxygen.

It was not until the following morning that I was allowed to hold either of my daughters. I always and still do feel sad that I didn't get to hold my babies until the next day. I was also told that it would not be safe for me to have any more children.[19]

As you can see, though our cesarean birth was absolutely needed, we still experienced many negative side effects from the cesarean itself. My sister experienced many breathing difficulties (which resulted in severe childhood asthma) even though she was full term and weighed well over six pounds. I never learned to nurse well and had poor weight gain. We were separated from our mother for an entire night before she was ever able to hold us. These are all common risks associated with cesarean birth and can sometimes contribute to long-term difficulties.

But the most notable side effect was that our mother had a stroke when we were born. Recovering from a stroke and a cesarean and learning how to take care of two babies all at once was quite an ordeal for her. She has also had to deal with lifelong side effects from her stroke since giving birth to us. If her cesarean hadn't been absolutely needed, those effects would have been truly burdensome—too great, even. Sadly, many women today are bearing these burdens when they could have achieved a vaginal birth. The overuse of cesareans greatly harms women and infants.

Fetal Malpresentation: Almost 4 percent of pregnancies will have a breech presentation, meaning that the baby's head is up toward the ribs instead of down in the pelvis. Currently, more than 85 percent of women with breech presentation will have a cesarean, even though there is a medical procedure that can help a baby flip and descend into the pelvis. This procedure is called an external cephalic version, and most women who receive a version will go on to deliver vaginally. Research shows that versions are underutilized, and ACOG is now encouraging doctors to offer their patients this procedure.[20]

External cephalic versions can be painful and often require pain medicine.[21] Many women try natural alternatives before agreeing to a version. Chiropractic adjustments boast an 82 percent success rate in getting breech babies into a head down position.[22] Exercises and body movements can also encourage a baby to descend head down. Should a baby remain head up, mothers can choose to attempt a vaginal birth or plan a cesarean. Both of these birthing scenarios carry greater risk than a normal vaginal delivery.

Fetal Distress: Obviously, if an unborn child is in true fetal distress, a cesarean is warranted. There are no natural alternatives or cures. However, fetal distress has a broad definition and is open to care provider interpretation, which leads to much variability.[23] Many concerning heart rate patterns can improve when a mother is able to change position or when the care provider uses techniques to stimulate the fetus.[24] You know from earlier in the book that inductions often lead to fetal distress, and that risk grows when an epidural is added to the equation. Mothers who avoid induction and pain medications are that much more likely to avoid this scenario.

Labor Dystocia: The most common reason for a care provider to suggest a cesarean is also the least clearly defined reason. With labor, there is no automatic cut off time, so it is up to the care provider to decide when labor is taking too long. Patience is definitely a virtue when it comes to giving birth. New research indicates that labor is longer than previously believed and that women are more likely to have a vaginal birth when they are given more time to labor.[25] Labor is not a race. Just because a woman hasn't given birth in a certain amount of time does not mean that she will not be able to give birth.

A long labor is not an evidence-based reason for receiving a cesarean. The risks associated with a cesarean are much higher than the risks associated with being patient. I have witnessed several providers offer cesareans to women whose labors were taking a long time to progress. Often, this makes a woman feel like the doctor is telling her that she needs a cesarean, which is not the case. If receiving a cesarean is a matter of life or death, your provider will not take the time to talk to you about it; remember that if there is time to discuss, it is not an emergency

Ways to avoid cesarean due to labor dystocia include laboring at home as long as you feel comfortable with, avoiding induction, avoiding pain medication, and utilizing natural methods proven to stimulate contractions. Walking, squatting, kissing, nipple stimulation (manual or by using a breast pump), and massaging pressure points are all great ways to speed up labor by increasing the natural production of oxytocin, all without any negative side effects.[26]

Interestingly, many of the most proven reasons for performing a cesarean do not make the top of the list, when they should be the only reasons on the list. (And notice that the number one reason cesareans are performed is not an evidence-based scenario!) Some of the most proven situations that require cesareans include problems with the placenta and problems with the umbilical cord. Although rare, the placenta can attach in an area of the uterus that would make the placenta be delivered before the baby. This is called placenta previa. It is life threatening to the child and absolutely requires a cesarean birth.

Cord prolapse is another situation that can be life threatening to the baby. It occurs when the umbilical cord exits the birth canal before the baby does. This can happen when the water breaks if the baby's head is high and not engaged in the pelvis. How low the baby's head is should be seriously taken into consideration when you or your care provider are considering breaking the water artificially, as cord prolapse can be a result of having your water broken.

PATIENCE AND LONG-SUFFERING IN CHILDBIRTH

Unfortunately, all births are not created equally. Some women will spend a handful of hours bringing their children into the world, and others will spend a handful of days. All births are difficult and trying, but some are just downright marathons. During these unusually long births, it is typical for a doctor to offer interventions to help speed things along, or to even offer a cesarean. But a long birth doesn't have to equal a birth filled with intervention.

For example, my twin sister, Hilary, was in labor with her one child longer than I was with all four of mine combined! My poor womb-mate was dealt a really hard hand with her first birth. And unfortunately, she and I were living too far apart from each other for me to be her doula. We spent a lot of time on the phone during the first hours of labor. Early on she could tell that her baby was posterior (meaning her baby was positioned incorrectly in the pelvis, causing much back pain and keeping her progress very slow). It is common. I personally have never had a posterior baby, but I have supported many women who have, and it's not easy. Throughout her labor she did everything she could think of to get her child into a better position, but Ruby was stubborn! The hours began to drag on and on. I would occasionally get a text from her husband asking for advice.

From experience I know that it can take a long time to get a first baby here. I tried not to worry, and it took all of my self-control not to pester them with texts asking for more information. But after many hours, even I started to worry that something had gone wrong. It had been six hours since I had last heard from them, and at that point she was at nine centimeters. I eventually assumed that she had ended up with a cesarean. I was shocked when I got the text that she had had a vaginal delivery with no intervention.

I was called to a birth for a doula client just minutes within getting the news of my niece's birth, so I was unable to call my sister the day she gave birth. Typically, Hilary and I speak several times a day, and I began to worry about her when she hadn't felt well enough to speak with me for several days.

When we finally talked, I could tell that she was beyond exhausted. The rigor of her labor had made her lose her voice. She was hanging on by a thread. She did not speak of the birth high. I don't think she even felt it. I feared that her natural birth had not been a good experience for her. And on top of that, her baby was lip tied and tongue tied, and nursing was going horribly. She was not experiencing any of the benefits you would expect from a natural birth.

But there *were* two enormous benefits she did receive, in spite of how difficult her birth was. First, enduring to the end of her labor showed her that she could also endure to the end with her breastfeeding struggles. Second, she had accomplished a vaginal birth, paving the way for future successful birthing experiences.

Hilary and her daughter's breastfeeding struggles continued for months. Hilary would call me crying (and in all our years together growing up, I think she cried twice), about to give up. I would typically encourage her to stick with it, but at times I felt she would be totally justified in quitting. It was so painful for her—and not the typical discomfort many mothers report. She would blister and bleed and peel. It was awful. But she had faith, and she had strength. She was magnified. Like a birthing mother who focuses on the relief in between contractions instead of the pain during them, Hilary focused on the good days of breastfeeding. Her good days got her through her bad days, and just when she thought it was too hard, it got better. To this day, I have never seen a woman overcome so much to breastfeed her child. After a long and painful six or seven months, nursing became a blessing and wonderful experience for her and her daughter.

As a doula, I have supported several women with almost the exact labor as my sister—a posterior baby, extremely slow progress, and plenty of discouragement. Eventually, all of my clients chose epidurals, and all of them received cesareans. I know that my sister's choice to avoid pain medication is what made the difference. Was it difficult? Extremely. Did she enjoy her birth? I doubt it. Has she ever regretted it? Not even for a second.

The future will be different for my sister than it will be for my clients. Since initially writing this chapter, my sister has given birth to her second child. Since she delivered vaginally with her first baby, she continued to be seen as low-risk. She did not have to worry about finding a provider who would allow her to try for a VBAC or have to deal with the uncertainty of being able to achieve a vaginal birth or not. She went into her second birth with the faith that she could deliver her child, and she knew from her past birth that she was strong enough for whatever would come her way. Her second birth was much shorter than the first, and she reaped many benefits of a natural delivery.

Sometimes the truest form of compassion we can show a birthing mother is giving her body more time to deliver her baby and giving her emotional and physical support throughout. By doing so, we can drastically decrease cesareans, morbidity, and mortality rates.

My sister's care provider showed true compassion by supporting her natural birth and allowing it to progress slowly. Even without intervention, some aspects of her labor would have warranted a cesarean under many opinions. Having an obstetrician that trusted the birthing process, was patient, and encouraging when my sister found herself doubting her ability to give birth will have a positive, long-term effect on my sister's future births.

VAGINAL BIRTH AFTER CESAREAN (VBAC)

Almost half of my doula clients are expecting their second or third child and have sought out the support of a doula due to their negative perceptions of their first birth—they want a different, and hopefully more positive, experience. Many of these women have had cesareans and hope to have a vaginal birth with their subsequent pregnancies. Like many birth scenarios, there are many misconceptions regarding VBACs and their safety.

Because we know that the cesarean rate is too high and that many cesareans are performed for unproven reasons, we can safely assume that many women who receive cesareans are still capable of giving birth vaginally. Due to the many difficulties women and infants experience from cesarean birth, many women desire to try to deliver vaginally with subsequent pregnancies after receiving a cesarean for a previous child.

The American College of Obstetrics and Gynecology states that successful VBACs have fewer complications than repeat cesareans and that approximately 60 to 80 percent of women who try for a VBAC will have a successful vaginal birth.[27] In a nutshell, VBACs are *safer* than cesareans, and most women are capable of giving birth vaginally.

Many hospitals and care providers do not support VBACs, even though ACOG states, "Our primary goal is to promote the safest environment for labor and delivery, not to restrict women's access to VBAC. The College says that restrictive VBAC policies should not be used to force women to undergo a repeat cesarean delivery against their will."[28] VBACs are not available to all women, and many women in the United States are forced to have repeat cesareans despite ACOG's clear message that VBACs are safer than cesareans and should be available to all healthy candidates.

Of course, some women will not be able to achieve a VBAC. Each case should be considered on an individual basis. But during my years as a doula, I have only had two VBAC clients require a second cesarean. Though disappointed, these women both knew that they had exhausted all of their options and done their best to avoid intervention. This brings peace of mind and birth satisfaction. All of my successful VBAC clients report a much higher birth satisfaction with their VBAC and also speak of recovering much faster with a VBAC. A vaginal birth after a previous cesarean is a safe option for most women and contributes to better birth outcomes.

Benefits of Avoiding Interventions

You and your baby are most likely to thrive when your birth is peaceful and free from unnecessary manipulation. Your baby is much less likely to experience the typical problems that newborns experience (breathing difficulties, nursing difficulties, inability to regulate body temperature, excessive fussiness, and injury due to a forced delivery) when your body goes into labor on its own and you are able to deliver your child without intervention.

I often hear women say, "As long as we are both alive and healthy at the end, that's all that matters." And they are right. But what is the definition of healthy? Having a live, healthy birth doesn't always guarantee the kind of outcome mothers are thinking of when they talk about being alive and healthy. For example, from a "healthy" birth you can find babies who can't nurse because their bodies are too tired from an adult dose of narcotics in their bloodstream, a mother who can't lift her child due to a surgical birth, a mother who received a vaginal injury from a delivery using forceps, or a baby who was cut during a cesarean and got a staff infection. Yes, both mother and infant have lived through the birth and will most likely recover and experience health in the future. But women can—and should—expect more than just living through the experience.

With our understanding and resources for childbirth, high morbidity rates from birth should not be socially acceptable today, but they are. While morbidity cannot be removed entirely, this chapter illustrates how easily it can often be avoided.

The scientific evidence clearly shows that God designed birth to unfold a certain way. When we alter His plan for birth, we put ourselves and our children at risk for many unwanted side effects. Too many women and infants are experiencing ill effects of births gone wrong. This doesn't have to be the case. While a natural birth is more challenging in the short term, the long-term benefits are often well worth the effort.

Below is a chart to help you remember some basics facts about when a cesarean is truly warranted.

EVIDENCE-BASED REASONS TO RECEIVE A CESAREAN	UNPROVEN REASONS TO RECEIVE A CESAREAN
Baby is in a position that makes a vaginal delivery impossible or dangerous	Large Baby
	Previous cesarean
Placenta Previa (When the placenta covers the cervix and would be delivered before the child)	Long labor
	Convenience
	Fatigue
Fetal distress	
Prolapsed cord	
Maternal illness such as active herpes or HIV	

NOTES

1. Luz Gibbons et al., "The Global Numbers and Costs of Additionally Needed and Unnecessary Caesarean Sections Performed per Year: Overuse as a Barrier to Universal Coverage," *World Health Organization*, World Health Report: Background Paper, no. 30, (2010).

2. Ibid.

3. Carol Sakala and Maureen P. Corry, *Evidence-Based Maternity Care: What It Is and What It Can Achieve* (New York: Milbank Memorial Fund, 2008), 44–46.

4. "Safe Prevention of the Primary Cesarean Delivery," *ACOG*, March 2014.

5. Sakala and Corry, *Evidence-Based Maternity Care.*

6. Ibid.

7. "Safe Prevention of the Primary Cesarean Delivery."

8. Sakala and Corry, *Evidence-Based Maternity Care.*

9. "Safe Prevention of the Primary Cesarean Delivery."

10. Ibid; Finding out the cesarean rate of a single hospital is often difficult, but you can find your state's cesarean rate here: http://www.acog.org/Resources_And_Publications/Obstetric_Care_Consensus_Series/Safe_Prevention_of_the_Primary_Cesarean_Delivery.

11. "Epidural and Spinal Anesthesia Use During Labor: 27-state Reporting Area," *CDC* 59, no. 5 (2011).

12. Sakala and Corry, *Evidence-Based Maternity Care.*

13. "Safe Prevention of the Primary Cesarean Delivery."

14. Ibid.

15. Ibid.

16. Ibid.

17. Ibid.

18. Ibid.

19. Valerie Ingoldsby

20. "Safe Prevention of the Primary Cesarean Delivery."

21. Ibid.

22. Heather Yost, "Turn Turn Turn: Options for Turning and Birthing Breech Babies," *Chiropractic For Life* 28 (2010).

23. "Safe Prevention of the Primary Cesarean Delivery."

24. Ibid.

25. Ibid.

26. Penny Simkin et al., *Pregnancy, Childbirth, and the Newborn* (Minnetonka, Minnesota: Meadowbrook Press, 2001) 263–65.

27. "Ob Gyns Issue Less Restrictive VBAC Guidelines," *ACOG*, July 2010.

28. Ibid.

Section Two

WORKSHEET

What surprised you the most about this section?

Was there anything you read that was frightening or hard to believe? Why?

Does having an understanding of common birth interventions make you more or less likely to use them? Why?

Did your beliefs about birth interventions change after reading this section?

Which intervention(s) are you most likely to still want? Which intervention(s) are you most hoping to avoid?

Section Three

MAKING BIRTH DECISIONS

*W*hile there is no doctrine dictating how a woman should give birth, there is ample doctrine on gender, gender roles, treating our bodies as temples, strengthening the family, and making choices that lead to optimal health and agency. For me personally, these areas of doctrine and guidance supported and encouraged my desire for natural birth, as giving birth encompasses and affects all of these areas.

Doctrinal truths, scientific truths, and promptings from the Spirit should all be taken into consideration when making any decision, including decisions about your birth. No two births are alike, and similar conditions will lead to different outcomes between women. For one woman, an induction and an epidural will lead to a quick and simple birth. For another, an induction and epidural will lead to an emergency cesarean and postpartum depression. There is no way of knowing beforehand which woman you are. The only thing we really *know* is that God designed childbirth, and that natural birth has the lowest instances of morbidity and mortality.

However, I also know that many women do not want to give birth naturally. No one wants risks or morbidity, but to some, the pain of giving birth is as frightening as the potential risks incurred while relieving pain. So how do we decide which path to take? Which decisions to make? Especially when we know that even in a natural birth, there is the possibility of needing to make difficult decisions.

Chapter 6

HOW DO I DECIDE?

*M*aking informed and inspired choices begins well before labor has started. Though not speaking about birth specifically, we can apply the following advice from Ezra Taft Benson: "Decisions should be based on correct principles and facts. A thorough knowledge of the principles and facts surrounding any particular problem usually leads to an easy and correct decision."[1] After reading chapters 4 and 5, you now have adequate information to begin making informed decisions concerning your births.

It is wise to go into your birth with an idea of what you are open to and what you aren't. You should know why you feel that way. An educated couple goes into their birth knowing how to make informed decisions and understands that the medical solution isn't always the only solution. But they also understand that sometimes it can be the best solution. They know what they want and why they want it, but they also know that flexibility may be necessary.

Many couples I speak with tell me they didn't feel they had a choice when it came to interventions in their births. And, yes, sometimes they may not have a choice in the matter. When an intervention is needed, the choice is already made. Other times, the choice is made because earlier choices have taken away agency to make different choices as labor progresses. And still other times, couples feel that they must agree to what their care provider suggests, assuming that there is no other choice. This is due to the authority mentality we experience in a medical setting; we often automatically assume that we must obey our doctor, but in reality, doctors are offering choices.

Your doctor may assume that you want to be induced and receive an epidural because the majority of the doctor's patients choose that path. Your doctor may assume that you would like a cesarean when your labor is progressing slowly. You, however, do not have to choose this.

Do not be afraid to speak up and ask questions. If there is time to ask questions and think things over, then what you are being offered is a choice. If you do not make the choice or know how to make the choice, then someone else will make it for you. You have the right to use your agency to direct your low-risk birth.

An acronym many childbirth educators use to help their patients make informed choices is BRANCH.[2]

Benefit: What do we gain by choosing this intervention?

Risk: What risks are commonly associated with this intervention?

Alternative: What else can we try before we choose this intervention?

Nothing: What happens if we do nothing?

CHoice: Relaying to your care provider what *your* choice is.

While not included in traditional childbirth education, I like to separate the c and the h.

Holy Ghost: Pause for spiritual confirmation.

Tuning into the Spirit is the final part of decision-making. This step is extremely beneficial when making difficult choices during pregnancy and birth. After you have gathered all your information *and* made your choice, don't forget to pause and listen for the whisperings of the Spirit. The Holy Ghost is ever available to you. Even in a high-stress situation, the Spirit will find a way to communicate with you because God loves you and cares about your birth. I have witnessed many couples be magnified by the Spirit during intense moments, and I have observed that the strength of impressions from the Holy Ghost will match the intensity of the situation to ensure that guided inspiration is available to those who seek it.

The Lord desires to help us discern between safe and dangerous choices. And what is safe for one birth could be dangerous for another. Sometimes informed and inspired choices will lead to a birth with more interventions than what the couple was hoping for. But more often, these choices will lead to naturally occurring births with low intervention use. Natural birth provides couples with the highest amount of agency. However, natural birth does not mean that there won't be difficult choices to make.

I remember attending a long birth of a first-time mom. She progressed much more slowly than would be expected, but she handled it very well. She remained optimistic and was able to make it to pushing without any intervention at all. After she had pushed for quite some time, it was clear that her skin was not stretching as much as would be expected. Her care provider expressed his concern that if she continued to push and deliver her baby without an episiotomy, her skin and muscles would most likely tear extensively. He offered her an episiotomy but allowed her to choose between receiving one or delivering her baby on her own and seeing how her body handled it.

We quickly used "BRANCH" to help her determine what she desired.

Benefits: Baby would most likely be delivered on the next contraction. Repair would be simple.

Decreased risk of tearing into the urethra.

Risk: Soreness, stitches (which would most likely be present in her situation anyways), and possible infection.

Alternative: Keep pushing and see what happens.

Nothing: Same as alternative.

Choice: This woman chose to receive an episiotomy, and quickly delivered her baby during the next contraction. She never thought she would have agreed to an episiotomy, as most women desire to avoid this intervention. But her natural labor and informed choice to receive one allowed her to have the best-case scenario for her particular birth.

Sometimes our birth choices lead to a medical outcome that we previously wished to avoid, and sometimes they lead to a birth many would think is impossible. A remarkable example is of one of my dearest friends, Emily. Emily and I met when we started dating our husbands. They were roommates at Ricks College (BYU–Idaho to all you young readers), and from that moment on, she and her husband became an important part of my life. As luck would have it, about five years after my husband and I were married, we moved to the same town Emily and her husband were living in. We did everything together. We even managed to have almost all of our children within days of each other; our sons were born four weeks apart from each other.

Emily had an epidural with her first three children. While she never had a horrible birthing experience, she never had an amazing one either. As she approached the birth of her fourth child, and after several discussions with me, she could easily see the benefits of a natural birth and desired to have one with this baby. The plan was for her and her husband to take my childbirth education class and for me to be their doula.

Our concurrent pregnancies turned out to be very different. I remember anxiously waiting to hear from her after her ultrasound. She was convinced she was having a girl. But having just found out that I was having a boy, I was really hoping she would have a boy too. I waited and waited to hear from her. The day dragged on and on, and I was getting a pit in my stomach. It wasn't normal to wait for a phone call from her. We talked on the phone almost daily. I ended up having to leave the house and had a message from her when I came home. I knew something was wrong the moment I heard her voice on the answering machine.

"It's a boy, and he's very sick." I could hear her trying to speak through her tears. It was horrible. Heartbreaking. Exactly how you don't want to feel after an ultrasound. She had just learned that her son had spina bifida.

Emily's birth plans changed quickly when the doctor told her she would need to deliver via cesarean section. Compared to everything else going on, this was a small blow, and she really didn't think much about it at first. As time went on, Emily began to feel that her fragile infant would benefit from a natural labor and birth, maybe even more than a healthy forty-week infant would. Why subject her son to an intervention-filled birth when he would already be subjected to surgery and anesthesia within hours of his birth? Surely, she thought, starting his life out naturally would give him some sort of help along the way. After receiving a second opinion from a different obstetrician and from talking to me, she firmly believed that giving her son a natural birth would be a great gift. She weighed the risks and benefits of each scenario and then knelt down and asked Heavenly Father if a vaginal birth would be safe for her and her son. The answer was "yes."

In the wee hours of the morning, I received the call that Emily was heading to the hospital to deliver her son. Since her second opinion came late in her pregnancy, she had missed the opportunity to attend my childbirth education class, so I didn't know what to expect from her. When

I spoke to her on the phone, I could tell she was well into her labor, and part of me wondered if she would have ordered her epidural before I could even get there. Either way, I hung up the phone, nursed my own four-week-old son, and headed downtown.

Her labor was fast and furious. Her son was born several hours after I arrived—vaginally, with no intervention. He slipped into the arms of a young resident (who looked thoroughly terrified that the OB on-call didn't arrive in time), and was quickly whisked away to be prepped for surgery. Emily got to reach her hand into the incubator and touch him once before they were separated. Knowing her son was heading into a major surgery, she whispered, "Come back to me."

Her husband went with their baby, and after several minutes it was just her and me, alone in an empty hospital room that was supposed to be filled with the sound of a newborn crying. I expected us to hold each other and cry. I leaned over her and hugged her. She sniffed once and pushed me away. I quickly realized that I was the one who wasn't strong enough for this moment. I was blown away by her strength. Where did it come from?

Remember how many women feel like they can do anything after they deliver naturally? Emily was now prepared to face some of the most difficult moments of her life with an oxytocin high. That, along with support from the Spirit, gave this mother the strength to see her baby taken away from her. She had a high-risk pregnancy, and her son required a long and difficult surgery within hours of being born. But there was one thing that was "normal" that she could choose. She could bring this child into the world safely, and the only help she needed was the Lord's.

Emily's son handled his surgery amazingly well. He breastfed easily, even though he wasn't allowed to nurse for several days. Emily feels that his healthy birth assisted in all of his early success. He continues to succeed today and is even walking, running, and completely potty trained! Many miracles came from that birth.

If You Need It, You Want It!

Always remember that no matter how much you hope to avoid intervention, at times intervention is necessary. This can be a difficult thing to accept for a couple who was well prepared for a natural birth. Over the years, I have had several clients who benefitted greatly from medical interventions, even though they initially did not want them. Most eventually realized how necessary the intervention was and agreed to it, despite their personal disappointment. But there are a few who never fully consented. Their desire for a natural birth clouded their judgment so much that they felt all intervention was bad, even when they truly needed it.

To these clients I always say, "If you need it, you want it!" All interventions used prudently and purposefully are wanted, even for those who hope to not need them. Refusing something that your birth needs is not helpful, and could possibly be dangerous. The easiest way to determine if interventions are truly needed is to go into labor on your own and avoid all interventions. When hurdles arrive in a natural birth, there is no need to wonder if an optional intervention led to another intervention. The distinction is clear, and there are no "what ifs."

If you are hoping for a natural birth but find yourself requiring intervention, remember that requiring intervention is not a failure. It is not indicative of you not being good enough. It is indicative of mortality. The design of childbirth is perfect, but our mortal bodies are not.

CHOOSING YOUR CARE PROVIDER

Clients often ask me about the differences between doctors and midwives. Both are highly skilled and trained professionals, qualified to assist and support low-risk births. However, obstetricians are specialized in the pathology of birth (which gives them the added expertise needed to attend high-risk births), while midwives are trained in the normalcy of it. This variation in training causes each profession to view and support birth quite differently. Midwives are typically trained to view birth as a healthy life event, which leads to a different type of care. Low-risk care does not encompass cesareans, leading midwives to discourage the use of unneeded intervention—interventions that often lead to cesareans—and offer natural alternatives.

Midwives assist births in hospitals, birth centers, and homes. Medically speaking, prenatal care from a midwife is identical to the prenatal care an obstetrician would provide to a low-risk patient. However, midwives tend to spend more time with their patients during prenatal appointments, which often leads to a closer and more trusting relationship. Women who choose midwifery care can always get the advice or assistance of a doctor if they have a concern that is outside of the midwife's scope or practice (changing their circumstances from low-risk to high-risk). Many women have expressed worry that hiring a midwife means not getting appropriate care should a complication arise. This is not true. Midwifery is a licensed profession, and in order to continue practicing, midwives must transfer care should a concern appear that they are not qualified to care for. Studies show that midwives provide the same high-quality prenatal care that doctors do and have much lower intervention rates.[3]

The biggest difference between doctors and midwives is that doctors are qualified to support high-risk births and perform cesareans. Studies on out-of-hospital midwives show that they have the lowest cesarean rates (usually between 4 percent and 5 percent) and that their outcomes are just as good as hospital outcomes. Hospital midwives have higher cesarean rates than out-of-hospital midwives (I assume this is due to the fact that they have access to interventions like inductions and epidurals), and obstetricians have the highest rates.[4]

Should you choose to give birth under the care of a physician, it is important to remember that the doctors and nurses who will be with you when you give birth are medical specialists. Many of my clients expect their care provider to offer natural alternatives, but that is rare. If you desire a provider who will offer this type of support, a midwife is probably a better fit for you. Others will choose to deliver under the care of a doctor but also hire a doula to offer physical support and give natural alternatives to the medical interventions that are offered at a hospital. Studies even show that having a doula present at a birth decreases the odds of cesarean by 28 percent![5]

Your choice of a care provider is a personal one, but a choice that may have long-term ramifications. In conjunction with the choices you make during your labor, your care provider's practice style will greatly influence the outcome of your birth and how medical or natural it will be.

The choice is not as much about choosing between a doctor or a midwife, but more about choosing a care provider you trust—someone who views birth the same way you do—and choosing a birth location that makes you feel most comfortable. Statistically speaking, though, if you do not want a cesarean, you are much less likely to receive one if you choose a midwife.

Choosing Your Birth

By understanding common interventions, you now have the power to exercise agency throughout your pregnancy and birth. You have the ability to discern what is prudent and what is not. You also have enough information to understand what type of birth is desirable for you and what you want to avoid the most. Women who feel that they were given choices during their births have higher birth satisfaction than those who felt manipulated or forced.

Remember that your birth is *your* birth and yours alone. Your choices only affect you and your family, so your decisions should not be based on what others think you should do. The opinions and preferences of others actually have no bearing on your birthing experience. It doesn't matter if you are the only one from your childbirth education class that gets an epidural, or if you are the only one in your Relief Society who had a natural birth. No one knows better than you do which type of birth will be most satisfying for you, and no one else is as entitled to personal revelation regarding birth decisions as the mother and the father.

The informed and inspired choices you make in your birth will not only improve your birth, but it could also pave the way for better care for others. Remember, there is no hierarchy in birth. You, your nurse, your care provider, and your Father in Heaven all have the same goal of a healthy birth. Different paths all eventually lead to the birth of a baby. You are allowed to choose your path, regardless of whether or not it is the path that is commonly chosen.

See Appendix C for more information on choosing which type of birth you desire.

NOTES

1. Ezra Taft Benson, "Principles of Decision Making," *Principles of Leadership: Teacher Manual Religion 108R*, (Salt Lake City: Intellectual Reserve, Inc., 2001).
2. Kyndal May, *The Evolution of Confident Birthing i-Advocacy*, http://www .babybumpservices.com/sharing-trust/the-evolution-of-confident-birthing-i -advocacy/.
3. Carol Sakala and Maureen P. Corry, *Evidence-Based Maternity Care: What It Is and What It Can Achieve* (New York: Milbank Memorial Fund, 2008).
4. Ibid.
5. Penny Simkin, "Position Paper: The Birth Doula's Contribution to Modern Maternity Care," *DONA International*, 2012.

"A mother's nurturing love arouses in children, from their earliest days on earth, an awakening of the memories of love and goodness they experienced in their premortal existence. Because our mothers love us, we learn, or more accurately remember, that God also loves us."[1]

M. Russell Ballard

Chapter 7

PARTNERING WITH YOUR FATHER IN HEAVEN

I cannot think of a greater honor than to partner with God and His almighty power of creation. How blessed I feel to have an earthly body that not only serves my own spirit but that also grows, houses, protects, and nourishes children. What on this earth is as amazing as procreation?

We know from earlier chapters that the blessings of procreation begin when oxytocin strengthens our relationships with our spouse during physical intimacy. Our celestial marriage is continually strengthened as we try to conceive. Then our body undergoes many changes in order to create a life within us. While not always easy, this change in our physical body gives us nine months to bond with our child and prepare to turn our time, attention, and love to that child. Our pain tolerance grows, and we can find ourselves physically, emotionally, and spiritually stronger than we have ever been. Not only do our bodies reach their full physical potential, but our minds and spirits can as well. By reaching our potential and creating a life, we can begin to conceptualize the creative power of our Heavenly Parents. That testimony continues to grow with us as we raise our children in the gospel and continue to try to be like our Father in Heaven.

When I stop to ponder women's assignment to bear children, I am extremely humbled by it—and at times, overwhelmed. Yet I, along with most women, am trusted to do it in whatever manner I choose. God trusts me to make choices that will keep my children healthy, strong, protected, and safe. It is not a mantle to be taken lightly.

There is no other time than procreation when a couple can come so close to being Godlike. Because God created everything, we can assume that our desire to create is part of our desire to be like Him. We spend most of our earthly life creating, whether it be creating a family, a meal, a career, or something to add beauty to our homes. Each of these things are only small endeavors compared to the amount of creative powers we will someday receive. Our creativity fills us with joy, excitement, and a sense of accomplishment.

President Dieter F. Uchtdorf explained that "creation brings deep satisfaction and fulfillment" and that "we each have an inherent wish to create something that did not exist before."[2] He also taught that creating is one of the ways we seek and experience eternal happiness. And certainly, motherhood is one of our creative efforts. "If you are a mother," he said, "you participate with God in His work of creation."

During pregnancy and childbirth, parents partner with God and learn to be more like Him. But does our desire to be like Him influence the way we give birth? Are we utilizing childbirth as a way to grow closer to God?

Without the entire truthfulness of the gospel, we cannot understand the entire truthfulness of anything, birth being no exception. As LDS women we know the wonderful duty of motherhood. We use motherhood to grow closer to the Lord and to become more like Him and, I assume, more like our Mother in Heaven as well. But too often we wait until *after* our children are born to begin this journey, when motherhood actually begins at conception.

During the first few years of my childbirth career, I felt I was the only one who thought childbirth was spiritual and designed by a loving Heavenly Father. Recently, I have discovered more women are coming to the same conclusions as they learn about the value and benefits of childbirth. Mommy blogs and Facebook pages often cover the topic of natural childbirth, and LDS-influenced pages are growing in numbers.

One day I was browsing blogs and found a post from a high school friend who had just given birth to her fourth child. She wrote:

> I was asked by many, including my husband, "Why in the world would you want to give birth naturally?!" Those questions caused me to dig deep to figure out exactly why this was so important to me. Since I came pretty close to doing it naturally the last time (not really on

purpose) I knew the pain is incredibly intense, but I was sooo close. . . . There are lots fewer "what ifs" health-risk-wise doing it naturally of course, and that was a big motivation—for my baby to come into this world as safely as possible. And then the midwife said my recovery would likely be so much quicker without one, so there was that. But it was more. It went deeper. I wanted to fully experience childbirth in all of its raw beauty (and yes, pain). Our bodies are made to do this incredible feat, and thanks to modern technology it's so much safer than say, back in pioneer-women times when there was no choice.

Am I crazy? I asked myself that question a lot. I vacillated back and forth. I knew that either way I wanted to be committed because otherwise I knew I'd "give in" when the pain hit. Don't get me wrong, I'm not totally against pain meds, I had two great epidurals with our twins and then our daughter after that, but both times I came away feeling like I personally had been cheated. Like I missed out on something incredible. This time around it became a lot more spiritual in nature as well. I like to be in control, and I DON'T like pain, so putting this totally in God's hands became my way of coming closer to Him and personally sacrificing my will to His. This may not make sense to some, and having been on the other side, I get it. But I also became more committed and determined with each day, feeling like, with His help, I could do it.

We got to the hospital about 8:00 p.m. and I was dilated to six (thanks to a lot of yuckiness/contractions and a previous sleepless night)! Since that was where my will started to crumble with both other labors I was encouraged. They had to start my antibiotics right away because I was Strep B positive (again), but it was happening so fast, I just wasn't sure we had the needed four hours for it to get into my system, so I was a bit concerned. The pain was definitely getting intense, but with my concentrated breathing, the birthing ball, and my husband pressing on the pain points in my back it was doable. We had talked and prepared quite a bit together and I knew if this was going to work, I needed his full support. I had it, and he. was. amazing. He provided the perfect, unflagging emotional and physical support I needed and the love I have for him doubled because of this experience!

I moved to the shower, on the ball and that was my sweet spot. I had soothing music going, the lights down low and used lots of vocalization (something I previously did NOT think was "me" or something

I would use, but it helped immensely). Then the midwife showed up and she provided the other crucial element—someone who had been through this before, knew what signs to look for, and could see that light at the end of the tunnel and propel me toward it. At one point I plead with her, "Tell me I'm close . . . tell me I can do this." She did—and when I could see she meant it I resolved I could keep going, at least for the next contraction or two. . . . There were a few times I just wasn't sure I could keep going—contraction after painful contraction, especially when I made the mistake of thinking about the utter relief I felt after getting the epidurals the other times. My personal will and strength were crumbling, but at that point of desperation and nearly giving in, something changed.

I feel like God intervened for me and changed my frame of mind. Suddenly I no longer thought about whether or not I could do it. I just focused on doing it, one contraction at a time. That made all the difference. The midwife stepped out to get me some juice and as soon as she left, I knew something big was happening. I didn't get that "overwhelming urge" to push per se, but maybe that's just because I've never felt that particular sensation before. Either way, it was incredible and exciting and terrifying. My baby was so close! I moved to the birthing stool and entered a whole new realm of pain. However, this time it was welcome pain. More progressive, the-end-is-in-sight pain.

For some reason the pushing took longer than I thought (maybe just because this time I could *feel* all that was going on!), but really it only lasted about thirty minutes. Also, the baby's head crowning did feel rather "fiery," but I had blissful rest from the contractions. In fact, at one point I just wanted to do nothing because it felt so much better than when the contractions were so intense. Eventually some major pain kicked in again and "persuaded" me to keep pushing. The midwife had me reach down and feel his head (another thing I didn't think I would do!) and when I felt it the seconnd time, and could feel how much *more* head had come out; wow, that was just what I needed. One more push and we heard his beautiful cry at 10:33 p.m. on June 13th, an hour and a half from his "due" date (two and a half hours from when we got to the hospital)! I simply cannot describe the joy, overwhelming relief, and total thrill of that moment.

Pain is one of life's greatest teachers. It brings us closer to Him if we let it. During the excruciating pain of labor I felt Heavenly Father walked my path with me in an incredibly personal way. He tenderly filled me with feelings that I was a strong and beloved daughter of God, and that through these experiences He gives women the inexplicable opportunity to partner with Him in one of His greatest miracles of all—childbirth—in order that we might each grow to know Him better. Personal knowledge I gained from my choice to "give birth naturally" that I now wouldn't trade for any pain relief, anywhere.[3]

All mothers partner with God, but no woman has partnered more with God during her birth than Christ's mother, Mary. And while I think her birth was as physically trying as anyone else's, I assume that spiritually and emotionally it was very different. Knowing that she was carrying the son of God had to have influenced the way she viewed birth and how much she relied on the Lord during her birthing experience. But I think God is just as willing to support all of us through our births. We know that God is always reaching to us, but we must also reach to Him.

Relying on the Lord

As with all big decisions in your life, don't make a decision about your birth without consulting the Lord. Have a prayer in your heart and invite the Spirit into your birth. And if you are one of the women for whom birth truly doesn't unfold the way it is designed to, the Spirit will comfort you. You will be able to discern if what you are being offered is appropriate and necessary, and you will have the blessing of knowing that you did everything you could to prepare for an optimal birthing experience.

I love working with all of my doula clients. Each birth teaches me so much and strengthens my testimony of God's plan for the family. I especially enjoy the opportunities I have to work with LDS couples. We share a different bond because of our shared beliefs. One particular couple was preparing to have a VBAC, meaning their first child was born via cesarean and this time they were hoping for a vaginal birth. They were planning to have their baby at a birth center with a caring and highly experienced midwife. Though well past her due date, she did finally go into labor. I met with them at 1:00 a.m. and spent the next fifty-three hours with them, except for about a twelve-hour break I took when my back-up doula came in to offer support. (This birth was much longer than most births, so don't panic while you read about it!)

At first, everything seemed to be happening normally. Over time her contractions became more frequent and more intense. About ten hours after meeting with them, she began to show signs of going into transition. Her contractions were close to each other, and her legs began to shake. I alerted the midwife, and then her labor seemed to subside. The shakes went away and her contractions began to space out. She spent the next thirty-five hours dilated to a seven. (Again, let me emphasize that this is not normal.)

Thankfully, their baby was doing great! Even though mom and dad were both tired, hungry, and beyond discouraged, their child was handling the marathon like a true champion. But this couple was faced with a difficult decision. They could stay at the birth center and continue waiting for her cervix to finish dilating, or they could transfer to the hospital in the hopes that a little Pitocin would do the trick. The main risk with going to the hospital was getting another cesarean. But the risk of staying at the birth center was not knowing how much longer she could handle this on her own. They prayed fervently. Tearfully, she decided to transfer to the hospital. It was a hard decision because she had prepared so hard for this birth and she wanted a vaginal birth so badly. Her husband gave her a priesthood blessing to help her emotionally handle the way her labor was going.

We were still optimistic when we arrived at the hospital. The on-call doctor was extremely warm and supportive. But within minutes of receiving the Pitocin, her baby went into fetal distress. Her baby's heart rate plummeted so quickly and so low that not only did she need a cesarean; she needed an emergency cesarean. In a matter of seconds she was gone, and I was left alone in the hallway with an anxious father.

After the birth, I asked her if she was okay with how everything had turned out. Although she still wished she could have delivered her child without intervention, she explained that she knew she had made the right decision to come to the hospital. For whatever reason, she was unable to deliver her child on her own, and she was thankful that Heavenly Father helped get her where she needed to be. I was so amazed and moved by what she told me. She had the Spirit with her and the strength from her priesthood blessing. She partnered with God to get her child here, and because of that partnership, she didn't have any lingering regrets or disappointment.

When we partner with our Heavenly Father and put our faith in Him, we don't have to wonder if things could have gone differently. So many women look back on their births with what-ifs and wonder if they could have had a different outcome. What if I hadn't been induced? What if I hadn't asked for an epidural? What if we had tried something else before agreeing to a cesarean? When you plan for a natural birth, do everything you can to accomplish that goal, and make your decisions with the Lord; you can be assured that you will always end up with the best-case scenario for your particular birth. Most of the time, things will progress smoothly and go well. If they don't, you will know that you did everything you could.

NOTES

1. M. Russell Ballard, "The Sacred Responsibility of Parenthood," from an Education Week devotional address given on August 19, 2003, at Brigham Young University.
2. Dieter F. Uchtdorf, "Happiness, Your Heritage," *Ensign*, November 2008.
3. Jenna Dayton, "Our Little Rhett," The Cutest Blog on the Block, 2011, http://daytonfam.blogspot.com/2011/06/our-little-rhett.html.

Section Three

WORKSHEET

What kind of birth philosophy do you hope your care provider has? Why? What qualities are you looking for in a care provider?

Which type of birth (natural or medical) do you think you would prefer? Why?

What decision do you hope you won't have to make during your birth?

Do you trust that the Holy Ghost will help you make inspired choices? Why or why not?

How do you plan to strengthen your partnership with the Lord while you prepare to give birth?

Do you believe that the Lord will magnify you during your birth? Why or why not?

Section Four

How Birth Affects the Family

The obvious way a birth affects a family is the addition of a child. Most parents are typically prepared for this change as they have dreamed of a tiny infant napping on their chest, and sparkling eyes smiling up at them. Most parents are well aware of the sleep deprivation that comes from night feeds and colic. But many are not aware of how giving birth may affect the mother emotionally.

For many women, the way they feel about their birth will transfer into the way they feel about themselves. Women with positive birthing experiences are more likely to experience an increase in self-esteem and feelings of empowerment. These feelings can affect a woman's family in a very positive way, as she feels good about herself and confident in her abilities.

Women who did not feel that their births were a positive experience, or women who experienced difficult or traumatic births, are more likely to experience postpartum depression. As with any type of depression, postpartum depression can deeply affect a woman's family as she struggles with feelings of low self-esteem, sadness, frustration, irritability, and negativity.

"Bearing my testimony to the truthfulness of the Book of Mormon to all those groups of people who knew little about our church is the greatest experience, outside of childbirth, that I have ever had. I compare it to childbirth because as I bore my testimony I experienced a uniting of body and spirit that I have felt only while giving birth to my children. It is as if everything you own is united together."[1]

Afton J. Day

Chapter 8

EMOTIONAL OUTCOMES

*H*aving a healthy mom and a healthy baby is everyone's number-one birth goal. Physical health helps a family thrive, but mental and emotional health are just as important. Even though we typically focus on physical outcomes, birth will also have an emotional effect on a woman. Often, our emotional outcomes stay with us much longer than our physical outcomes do. Along with physical health, optimal emotional health should also be a goal of our plans for birth.

The oxytocin high experienced after a natural delivery aids in a woman's emotional well-being. The birth high helps a woman feel empowered, capable, excited, and overcome with love for her child and even her spouse.

EMOTIONS AFFECT THE FUTURE

When I was working on my bachelor's degree in music therapy, I spent a semester working with hospice patients. I really enjoyed this population. I worked with a patient named Ruth who was in her late nineties. While her body was old and failing her, her mind was still alert. I loved hearing her stories of getting picked up for dates on a horse instead of in a car. She also shared her birth stories, and she remembered so many details. I was amazed at how much she could remember about an event that took place seventy years ago. She gave birth at home, without intervention, and not once did she talk about how hard or painful it was. She remembered things like the weather and how long her labors lasted, but mostly she talked about what her children looked like and how she *felt*.

The way a woman feels after giving birth will contribute to how she feels in the future. If her birth made her feel strong, capable, joyful, and optimistic, she will take those feelings home with her. At home, those feelings and emotions will help shape the family environment. Sadly, if a birth makes a woman feel incapable, frustrated, scared, or angry, these feelings will also be brought home.

Along with the birth high, many variables factor in to how a woman feels emotionally about her birth. Was she treated with kindness and respect? Was she able to make her own decisions regarding her birth? Was there something she really wanted to experience while giving birth that she wasn't able to experience? Is there something from her past that would make giving birth emotionally difficult (sexual abuse, for example)? Was the birth chaotic and frightening, or was it peaceful? Even with a perfectly healthy baby, a woman may feel saddened by her birth. Conversely, a woman may give birth to a baby that needs much medical attention, but still have a wonderful emotional outcome from her birth.

EMPOWERMENT

I have found that if you get any group of women together, the topic of childbirth is bound to come up at least once per gathering. One particular evening, the topic of childbirth was running rampant as I was out with friends and just days away from delivering my third child.

I overheard one mom say, "I felt on top of the world, like I could do anything." After asking her what she was referring to, she told me that is how she felt after she delivered her last child without any pain medication or medical intervention. What could possibly be more empowering than feeling like you can do anything?

Heavenly Father knew that mothers would be tested and tried on a daily (okay, let's be honest—hourly!) basis. Mothers in Zion need the inner strength and belief that they can rise to any occasion required of them. Birth prepares women for this. Every woman who delivers her child naturally gets to the point in her labor where she believes she can't do it anymore. As miserable as that sounds, this is a wonderful event because soon thereafter she will prove herself wrong. By actually climbing the mountain that is not climbable, women are truly empowered because now they have to believe in themselves.

I believe that God designed childbirth to be difficult so the joy and sense of accomplishment from it would be overwhelming. Surely Heavenly

Father wants every new mom to go home feeling confident and ready to tackle the challenges of motherhood. These feelings of confidence and empowerment are seen more often in women who deliver their babies naturally, as they are often a result of the hormonal and endorphin birth high, as well as the self-esteem boost natural birth can provide. These mothers give themselves the credit, and that's a good thing! All too often I see women who have medical births giving all the credit to the medical staff. Even when medical intervention is used, it is still the mother who did the work! So many women fail to recognize how amazing their body and their ability to give birth is.

Just knowing that you are capable of bringing a life into the world should be empowering, but many women are leaving their births feeling incapable instead of empowered. For some it will be due to lack of oxytocin; for others it will be from the disappointment of not achieving the birth they desired, and possibly feeling that they weren't strong enough to cut it. Heavenly Father created *all* women to be strong enough to withstand childbirth, even those who are not given the opportunity to. The true empowerment comes from being a daughter of God and knowing that He has always believed in your ability to bring about mortal life.

EXCITEMENT AND BONDING

The birthing atmosphere will vary greatly depending on the type of birth a woman has. For many, it is impossible not to get caught up in the moment of a natural delivery. Even a dad who was somewhat disenchanted, uncomfortable, or drowsy during his wife's labor will zero in on the excitement of pushing. Men who swear they aren't going to look are suddenly announcing things like, "It's coming," "PUSH!" or, "I can see the head!" It is thrilling.

Oxytocin and endorphins are about to peak for the mom, creating a birth high (similar to how a runner feels after completing a marathon) and heightened bonding. The people around her will feed off of her oxytocin and make more themselves. Dad is so involved, his oxytocin is also rising, and before he knows it, he is cutting an umbilical cord. Both mom and dad are breathing heavily, finishing this marathon hand in hand.[2]

One woman recalls her own birth high like this: "I had heard that the hormonal 'high' after birth was the strongest biologically produced rush that a woman ever experiences and I was still surprised when I was still feeling blissful three days after my baby was born. He was sleeping away but I was awake and happy. In looking back at pictures from that time, my favorite is my baby snuggled against me sleeping. I look so peaceful and it matches exactly what I was feeling at the time. I fell in love with my baby in those early days and I am so glad to have photos documenting those special moments."[3]

It's not just oxytocin filling the room. I can strongly feel the presence of the Holy Ghost at every birth I attend. Couples have told me they would have another baby just to feel that way again. Most of my clients are not LDS, and they do not have a full understanding of why they feel so amazing after their baby is born. But the Spirit is there, and it is beautifully strong.

Physiologically speaking, the moments directly after birth will vary greatly between natural and medical births. Because oxytocin is not spiking after medical births, bonding will not be physiologically heightened. This does not mean that a woman who delivers with an epidural cannot feel joyful or connected to her baby. However, it often means that she will have to work a little harder to have those feelings. While emotions are quite heightened during a natural delivery, they can be quite dull during a medicated one. Just as medication disconnects the brain from the labor, it can also disconnect emotions from the labor.

I remember a particular birth in which the mom was so disengaged with her baby that when the nurse asked her if she wanted to hold her baby before they took him away to wipe him off and perform a newborn assessment, the mom said, "No, I just really want a milkshake." That might make you chuckle because it isn't what we expect to hear, but really think about that: a woman who has carried a child for nine months, has anticipated his arrival, has wondered what he would look like and what color his hair and eyes would be, isn't even interested when she finally gets to see him.

To help a woman stay physiologically connected to her baby and her labor, I encourage the use of prenatal bonding through music. I help my clients find music (typically lullabies) that helps them feel connected to their child during the pregnancy. By listening to this music during pregnancy and using it as a way to draw closer to their child, they are training their body to create oxytocin every time they listen to it. I then turn this music on shortly before the baby is born. This helps a mom who has been sleeping with an epidural quickly tune back into her labor. It also helps her body create oxytocin and heightens her emotions during and after the delivery.

The first few moments after birth can have a lasting effect on how parents feel about the birth of their children long-term. Once that moment has come and gone, you cannot re-create it. Parents who felt this moment with intensity will revel in it for years to come. It will influence the way they share their birth story their entire life.

STRENGTHENING MARRIAGE THROUGH BIRTH

God designed the hormonal releases that women should experience after giving birth. They were designed to benefit women, infants, and families. Oxytocin plays many roles in birth: it keeps labor progressing, aids in the production of breast milk, and fills a mother's brain with maternal instincts that help her bond with her baby and have a desire to protect it. Often those feelings of intense bonding transfer into the marriage, as husbands and wives find themselves loving their child, and each other, intensely.

Pregnancy and birth are both emotional experiences. Natural childbirth heightens our emotions and allows strong and intense bonding to occur in a relatively short period of time. When husbands and wives work together during this time of emotional intensity, their marriage can be strengthened.

A father's oxytocin levels will rise during the birth of his child, which will innately encourage him to bond with his child. Through bonding, a hormone called vasopressin will also be produced. Vasopressin helps a male feel dedicated to his spouse and child and brings out a man's protective role. While the more well-known hormone of testosterone contributes to a male's libido, vasopressin tempers a man sex drive and encourages monogamy.[4]

A close friend of mine felt this strengthening within her own marriage during the birth of their second child. Here is her explanation in her own words:

> During my second pregnancy, I told my husband, Seth, I wanted
> to have a natural birth. I'm not sure he entirely believed me at first,
> but we began attending Hypnobirthing classes to prepare. Over time,
> something changed in him, and I could tell he was truly on my team.
> He and I both really relate to childbirth being like a marathon in the

mental preparation, so throughout my pregnancy and birth we used that imagery. Seth deciding to be on-board strengthened our marriage more than I even fully recognized at the time. Having him decide to do it with me, and be 100 percent supportive, meant it would happen. I felt that with his support, I could do anything.

Seth was my rock, especially during my final week of pregnancy. I was more than ready to be done with pregnancy, and was very stressed about my dad's upcoming open-heart surgery. Seth filled that week with blessings, prayers, and words of comfort, in addition to the many walks we took to encourage labor to start. I can't imagine dealing with that alone. He listens, comforts, and walks on eggshells to do what it takes to get me to where I need to be.

When labor started in the middle of the night, Seth got up with me and helped me labor. He'd hold my hand and rub my back, and be present during each and every contraction. Somehow having him there eased the pain. It's probably very much like how the Atonement works in that when we have someone by our side it doesn't seem nearly as hard, because they can "take" some of that stress and pressure. Seth did that as much as he could with every part of our pregnancy, and it especially stood out in the labor and delivery part. He never left my side, physically or emotionally.

Seth also desperately tried to help keep me in control during the moments that I felt I was going to lose it! I'd grab his arm and hit his leg during some contractions, and he would not only take it, but encourage it if it helped me. He would listen to me cry, and physically hold me up during contractions. I feel closer to him because of his support and encouragement to help me accomplish something I really wanted to do. How could I not love him more after that was all over?[5]

Childbirth has the potential to strengthen a woman, and a marriage, spiritually and emotionally. When birth unfolds the way it was designed to, and when women are supported and given agency over their births, positive emotions are likely and self-esteem is supported. When birth is manipulated and women leave the experience feeling confused and unsupported, postpartum depression is also likely.

Notes

1. Afton J. Day, "Then I Could Touch People's Hearts," *Ensign*, September 1977.

2. Jennifer Block, *Pushed: The Painful Truth About Childbirth and Modern Maternity Care* (Massachusetts: Da Capo Press, 2007), 135, 172; Sarah Buckley, "The Hidden Risks of Epidurals," *Mothering* no. 133, November–December 2005.

3. Jenne Erigero Alderks, "Rediscovering the Legacy of Mormon Midwives," *Sunstone* no. 166 (2012).

4. Linda Folden Palmer, "The Chemistry of Attachment," *The Attached Family*, http://www.pregnancy.org/article/bonding-matters-chemistry-attachment.

5. Personal correspondence with Jane Price Johnson.

Chapter 9

POSTPARTUM DEPRESSION

After a woman gives birth, her estrogen and progesterone plummet.[1] These two hormones have been on overdrive during the pregnancy (causing all those wonderful mood swings and breakouts, but also keeping you pregnant). After the placenta is delivered, the hormones once keeping a pregnancy thriving are now depleted and are at much lower levels than before the woman was pregnant. This lack of hormonal balance causes many women to feel emotional, and many will find themselves crying with no apparent cause. This depletion of hormones leads 50 to 80 percent[2] of women to have the "baby blues."[3]

The baby blues should last no more than a week or two and resolve on their own as hormone levels balance out. Many women report feeling emotional during the first week or two after giving birth. You should not feel alarmed or overly worried if you find yourself experiencing swings of sadness or sensitivity.

For some women, these feelings of sadness will not go away on their own, and they will experience postpartum depression. Unlike the baby blues, postpartum depression is a serious medical diagnosis. It should be taken just as seriously as any other depression diagnosis. Postpartum depression affects up to 20 percent of new mothers, making it one of the most common side effects of giving birth.[4] However, this 20 percent is just the number of women who report having postpartum depression. After over a decade of working with women giving birth, I feel that 20 percent is a low estimate of how many women are actually coping with this.

Knowing that hormonal fallout would be a natural consequence to childbirth, Heavenly Father created a way to combat the low feelings caused by it. A combination of oxytocin, endorphins, and even a bit of adrenaline can help a woman remain emotionally balanced after the birth of her child. The birth high was not only designed to help a woman bond with her baby and feel good about herself, it was also designed to help balance out the estrogen and progesterone low so women can survive this hormonal rollercoaster.

All women will experience the dramatic drop in hormones after giving birth, while few will experience the after-birth high that was designed to help them overcome their hormonal fallout. Research suggests that a lack of oxytocin at the moment of birth contributes highly to not only the baby blues, but also postpartum depression.[5]

Research also indicates that higher occurrences of physical complications during birth lead to higher occurrences of women suffering emotionally after the birth.[6] Women are emotionally fragile after giving birth, especially if their birth was medicated, traumatic, or extraordinarily difficult.

However, hormonal fallout alone is enough for many women to experience postpartum depression. Since every woman experiences this after giving birth, every woman is susceptible. When you add in other factors, such as a difficult or disappointing birth, cesarean birth, lack of oxytocin, difficulty breastfeeding, difficulty bonding, fatigue, poor nutrition, lack of support, unrealistic expectations of motherhood, pressure to return to work quickly, marital stress, financial stress, or any other type of stress, postpartum depression becomes more likely. Natural birth can shorten the list of potential risk factors for postpartum depression but certainly does not remove all of them.

Many women with postpartum depression do not share their experiences with others. Imagine how difficult it would be for an LDS mother to admit that she does not enjoy being a mother. She may feel ashamed or worried that others will judge her. It is isolating to feel like the only woman who isn't happy since she became a mother. While much of our society is unaware of postpartum depression and its many ramifications, I have sadly observed and supported many women who have struggled with postpartum depression, and I have seen it destroy families. I have seen women under the influence of postpartum depression leave their husbands and abuse drugs. I have even spoken to several who contemplated taking their own lives. It is clear to see that postpartum depression can sometimes lead to decisions that can have an enormous, and even disastrous, impact on a family.

We know that Heavenly Father is aware of His children battling depression. Heartfelt expressions of compassion and concern have been delivered by apostles who have seen the effects of depression on the family, including women struggling with postpartum depression. In one such address, Elder Jeffrey R. Holland encouraged Latter-day Saints to prevent illness whenever possible, and pointed out that fatigue is often a strong contributor to depression. He advised us to slow down, rest up, replenish, and refill.[7] But fatigue is a given for new mothers, and the opportunity to slow down and replenish is often not there. Natural birth can help prevent the illness of postpartum depression, but it is no guarantee. Hormonal fallout and fatigue will be present for all women who give birth, and may lead to postpartum depression.

DEPRESSION IMPEDES BONDING

Sadly, almost one-third of women with postpartum depression will experience difficulty bonding with their baby.[8] It is important to understand that there is a difference between loving a child and bonding with them. Difficult bonding is seen in how a woman responds and reacts to her child, despite how much she loves her baby. Women who are indifferent or inhibited around their baby show subtle signs of struggling to bond.[9]

Bonding is key to God's plan for the family. Babies are born dependent and naturally bond to the person who takes care of their needs. Being with their caretaker makes babies feel calm, safe, and happy. Bonding should be emotionally positive for the baby and for the mother, and the mother-infant relationship should be mutually satisfying.[10] We can assume that God desires us to not only love our babies but also to bond with them since oxytocin is the key ingredient needed for birth, breastfeeding, and bonding.

Initial bonding, directly after birth, should feel natural and instinctual. As we discussed in chapter two, physiological labor and birth heightens bonding and a woman's maternal instincts. These hormones and instincts help make newborn care and breastfeeding feel natural, even desirable, even if the woman has never done them before. She instinctively wants to be close to her child and meet her child's needs. Our instinctual bond makes us crave closeness with our infants and put their needs and comfort as top priority. Despite the high needs of infants, caring for their needs brings the bonded mother joy and satisfaction. Women who do not feel drawn to their crying baby, or resent how much their baby needs from them, may be struggling to bond.

As difficult as it is to discuss, stressful births and low oxytocin levels at birth can hinder instinctual bonding.[11] This does not mean that a stressful or medical birth will ruin your relationship with your child. But it does mean that those types of births can make bonding more difficult—so much more difficult that 40 percent of first-time moms report feeling *nothing* towards their child the first time they hold them.[12]

These are important correlations to understand, as postpartum depression can lead to difficult bonding, and difficult bonding can lead to postpartum depression. It is a cycle that continues to feed into itself. Bonding has the potential of being intense and instantaneous. If this is not the case for you, don't panic! There are many things you can do to promote bonding with your child. Spending time together is key. Keep your baby close to you, preferably skin to skin. Give your baby a massage. Nap together and snuggle throughout the day. Look into their eyes when you feed them. Give yourself permission to slow down, live in the present, and just focus on your little one.

Most women I have worked with who were struggling with postpartum depression feel that they will be happier if they have less time with their baby. And, yes, every mom needs a break now and then, and definitely needs support. However, lengthy separation of mother and baby will not improve difficult bonding, and typically will not improve postpartum depression. Finding ways to improve the mother-infant bond and provide emotional support for the woman will render better results. A woman's attachment to her child should make taking care of her infant enjoyable and satisfying, and also ensures close proximity and met needs for the baby. Our physiological design makes babies prefer their mothers, and makes mothers want to stay close by and be readily available.

Satan Exploits Depression

Elder Robert D. Hales taught that "Lucifer was one of Heavenly Father's most brilliant spirit sons."[13] And though he never received a body himself, he has figured out how to use our own bodies, and their accompanying weaknesses, against us. Satan is well aware of the fragile state of a woman's body and mind during her pregnancy, birth, and postpartum period.

Through personal and professional experiences, I have seen firsthand how Satan desires to destroy the family, particularly around pregnancy and early parenting. I feel we can safely assume that he will look for opportunities to attack our families starting from the moment we discover we are pregnant. Perhaps he plants doubts in our mind about our ability to be good mothers or our strength to withstand childbirth. If he can get us to embrace enough fear, he will have crowded out our faith in the birth process and in ourselves.

I also assume that Satan knows that when the birthing process is altered, it increases a woman's risk to becoming depressed, doubting her ability to mother, and even struggling to bond with her children. He knows that if he can get a mother to doubt herself, it is less likely that she will be able to achieve her divine potential.

Ezra Taft Benson taught, "Satan is increasingly striving to overcome the Saints with despair, discouragement, despondency, and depression."[14] Satan is well aware that many women will experience depression after the birth of their child. He is also aware that he can often exploit that depression and turn it into resentment, inability to reach goals and potential, and even sin.

When we become depressed, it is difficult to feel the Spirit. When our lives lack the Spirit, it becomes easier to give in to temptation. Satan will prey on a woman experiencing postpartum depression, just as he preys on anyone with depression.

He will work to find ways to make the new mom focus on her sadness or frustrations, instead of the joy brought from her new child. He will exploit the lack of oxytocin and interfere with bonding as much as possible. He knows that if he can impede the mother-child bond, he will be able to continually tear her family apart. Because of his time in the premortal world, Satan understands the potential of the family unit. And he understands that if he has any chance of winning, it will be accomplished through the destruction of the family. He also knows that if he can break you down, you won't be able to raise anyone else up, including your children.

I want to be clear in stating that Satan and sin are not the causes of postpartum depression, and all women are susceptible to this trial. Struggling with depression is not a sign of unrighteousness. Many women will suffer from postpartum depression, *even with a natural birth*, and it is important for all couples to be emotionally and spiritually prepared for such an event. New mothers greatly benefit from the additional oxytocin, the support, and the constant presence of the Holy Ghost in a natural birth.

MY EXPERIENCE WITH PPD

We focus on the physical difficulty of giving birth, but birth is also demanding mentally, emotionally, and spiritually. Most likely, it will expose your weaknesses in some or all of these areas. If you are struggling particularly in one of these areas, you are likely to feel the effects of that struggle during your birth. Coping with weaknesses and trials is even more difficult when a woman is experiencing hormonal fallout, as well as fatigue from birth and early parenting.

As you recall from earlier in the book, I experienced difficult challenges during my early parenting years. While I was pregnant with my second child, I lost my father to cancer and my firstborn was diagnosed with a brain tumor. I went into my second birth emotionally broken. Out of all four of my births, I remember this birth to be the most difficult to bear, not because it was a difficult birth but because I was lacking in emotional and spiritual strength. I was also angry, especially with God. How could He take away my father and then threaten to take away my first baby at the same time?

I definitely felt the effects of hormonal fallout. With my first birth I felt the birth high for quite some time. It carried me through weeks of sleepless nights. It compensated for the hardship of caring for a baby with a strong temperament. But with my second birth, it wasn't enough. My low had become too low for even the birth high to pull me up. I was at the end of my emotional rope within days of giving birth. I would hear my baby cry in the middle of the night, and I would lay in my bed and cry too, because I didn't have the strength to tend to her needs. It was too much. I could no longer hold in my sadness and stress from my trials, and it quickly came crashing down on me. Even though I desperately loved my children and wanted to be a good mother, I couldn't be.

I began to resent how much my daughters required of me. Being only sixteen months apart, one of them always had a pressing need. As a result of being born too soon, my baby choked often, and my sixteen-month-old required much medical care. Something always kept me from doing anything for myself. I watched the clock all day, waiting until my husband could come home and help me. I began to resent him and the freedom he had. One day he told me he sat under a tree and read a book during his lunch hour and I was furious. How dare he do something enjoyable when I was stuck at home in my misery!

I could feel my testimony slipping away, and I didn't even care because I didn't have the strength to reach for it. The only time I prayed was to ask God why He hated me so much. Satan had convinced me that God did not care about me. He had successfully gotten me to resent my children, my husband, and my entire life. Months passed before I was able to feel the Spirit again.

It was a long road back. Some of my issues resolved on their own. As my baby stopped choking, my anxiety started to subside. As our sleep schedule improved, I was able to receive much needed rest. After my period returned, I felt that my hormones were more under control, and I was able to feel some joy again. I had loving friends and family members who allowed me to talk about the pain of losing my dad and the stress of medical procedures for my daughter who was recovering from brain surgery. But the longest resolution was restoring my testimony. Losing the Spirit does not resolve on its own. While not all women with postpartum depression will experience a loss of the Spirit, this was my personal trial and experience. But it is—and will continue to be—a struggle for some of the women battling postpartum depression.

This painful experience taught me that we need to be prepared for spiritual trials after birth and understand how susceptible we are not only to depression but also to Satan's influence. While a natural birth decreases your probability of experiencing postpartum depression, it does not guarantee that. It is, however, something you can be proactive about to reduce your chances of suffering it.

Many factors contribute to postpartum depression, and most we cannot control. In conjunction with hormonal fallout, stressful life events, a traumatic birth, a colicky baby, inadequate rest, poor nutrition, and lack of support all contribute to this condition.

COPING WITH POSTPARTUM DEPRESSION

As with any treatment plan, many paths lead back to optimal health. The key is finding the plan and path that works for you. Should the first thing you try not bring about desired results, try a new path. A diagnosis of postpartum depression does not have to ruin your life, your happiness, or your testimony.

First and foremost, remember that you are a daughter of Heavenly Parents who love and cherish you. They believe in you and have sent you a choice spirit that needs you to take care of yourself physically, emotionally, and spiritually. It is easy to doubt your ability to mother, but as long as you love your child and are meeting his or her physical needs, you are doing a great job.

When experiencing postpartum depression, adequate rest and healthy meals (particularly protein intake) are a *must*. These two things are also often difficult to come by in the early throws of newborn care. But they must be a priority because the lack of sleep and poor nutrition will only contribute to the problem.

Don't try to do everything on your own. In our society, there is so much pressure to resume normal living as soon as possible after giving birth. This is not realistic and puts way too much pressure on new parents. A friend of mine, who is also a postpartum doula, encourages her clients to stay in bed for the first week postpartum and hand over all tasks to other people for several weeks. The only job a new mom has is to feed her child. All other work should be done by someone else. This can be difficult for women who already have children or for women whose husbands cannot take much time off from work.

It is helpful to come up with a post-birth plan before you have your child. Line up play dates for older children, and get rid of all expectations of a clean house. It is okay to put rest before housework. When possible, it is extremely helpful to have a mother, mother-in-law, or sister come and stay with you after you have given birth. They should stay with the intent of cooking and cleaning for you, not holding the baby for you while you do the work.

If you need help, speak up. Everyone wants to be a super-mom, even though many other women would be more than happy to help and serve us when we need assistance. Don't be ashamed or embarrassed to tell your husband, close friends, visiting teachers, or Relief Society president that you are struggling and could use help with meals, running errands, or anything else that it too difficult to accomplish. Speak openly about your feelings with someone you trust. There is no need to carry the burden alone. Also, take your burdens and concerns to the Lord through fervent prayer.

If support, rest, and nutrition are not enough, it is time to seek professional help through a counselor, your care provider, or both. When breastfeeding, I would advise seeking a non-pharmaceutical treatment first. But of course, if that isn't enough, finding an anti-depressant is necessary. (And there are several approved to take while nursing.)

Make every effort to remain close to the Spirit. Continue to pray daily, sing Primary songs to your infant, and request priesthood blessings. Read your scriptures or listen to general conference addresses while you nurse. Do something that feeds you spiritually.

Remember—there is hope. While depression can feel like a downward spiral, it is a spiral that can be overcome.

Though all early parenting will have its stressful moments, God wants you to enjoy this time in your life. Creating a family is our earthly practice to start to become like Him. It is how we learn to love as He loves and serve as Christ did. There is nothing else on this earth that makes us more like God.

(See Appendix D for more information on diagnosing postpartum depression.)

Notes

1. "Depression during and after pregnancy fact sheet," *Womenshealth.gov*, http://www.womenshealth.gov/publications/our-publications/fact-sheet/depression-pregnancy.html.

2. Sema Kuguoglu et al., *Breastfeeding After a Cesarean Delivery*, ed. Dr. Raed Salim (2010), http://www.intechopen.com/books/cesarean-delivery/breastfeeding-after-a-cesarean-delivery.

3. Penny Simkin et al., *Pregnancy, Childbirth, and the Newborn* (Minnetonka, Minnesota: Meadowbrook Press, 2001), 377.

4. For more information, visit www.postpartum.net.

5. "Depression during and after pregnancy fact sheet"; *Postpartum Support International*, www.postpartum.net; Carol Sakala and Maureen P. Corry, *Evidence-Based Maternity Care: What It Is and What It Can Achieve* (New York: Milbank Memorial Fund, 2008).

6. Sarah Buckley, "The Hidden Risks of Epidurals," *Mothering* no. 133, November–December 2005; Henci Goer, *The Thinking Woman's Guide to a Better Birth* (New York: The Berkley Publishing Group, 1999), 134.

7. Jeffrey R. Holland, "Like a Broken Vessel," *Ensign*, November 2013.

8. Kuguoglu et al., *Breastfeeding After a Cesarean Delivery*.

9. Ibid.

10. Ibid.

11. Ibid.

12. Robert D. Hales, "I am a Child of God," *Liahona*, 1978.

13. Ezra Taft Benson, "Do Not Despair," *Ensign*, November 1974.

Chapter 10
RAISING THE NEXT
GENERATION OF BIRTHERS

*C*hildren are naturally curious about how babies get inside moms' tummies *and* how they get out! Many parents dread figuring out how to answer these innocent questions. It is important to remember that the feeling and substance of our answers can leave a lasting impression on our children and how they view childbirth.

Even though they may not understand everything they hear, children often listen to the adults who are speaking around them. Some of the most unexpected questions my children have asked me came directly after a playgroup where I assumed they were too engrossed in their toys and friends to be listening to me. Young mothers speak often of birth, and young children try to figure it all out as they piece together the few things they understand.

Because birth is difficult and misunderstood, most of what children hear concerning it is negative. Once you stop to notice what kinds of messages children are receiving, you realize there is much talk of the fear of childbirth, the pain of giving birth, and women and children dying during childbirth. For instance, how can a wicked stepmother enter the family if the mother did not die during childbirth? There are even frequent general conference talks where the purpose is to help us learn to overcome adversity, but they often include stories about the death of children or mothers due to childbirth. While these stories are useful for their settings in movies and talks, they also send an unintended message that childbirth should be feared.

If the only thing we hear about childbirth is that women and babies die, or that most women have horrible or painful experiences, it will greatly influence the opinions of women and young women on the safety of giving birth. Taking into consideration age-appropriateness, I always speak openly and honestly with my daughters about childbirth. I hope that my honesty and optimism will set the stage for success in their future. It certainly will serve them better than telling them how awful birth can be.

I was once asked to be on a panel of women in my ward for a special Young Women's activity. The goal of the evening was to share our education and careers with the young women, as well as how we balance work and family. I was excited to be a part of this event. Out of five women, I was second to last. When it was my turn to present, I began by explaining to them what a doula is and how I support women while they give birth. Quickly, the woman scheduled to speak after me told me not to scare the young women and then proceeded into her own presentation. I was so disappointed because I had had a chance to make a difference—to plant positive seeds in the hearts of our future mothers and inspire a young woman to look forward to giving birth. In an instant, that chance was gone because of the pervasive, negative attitude about birth in our culture.

Because their mother is a doula, my children seem to have an even greater interest in childbirth than the average child. Because of my work, childbirth seems like a much more normal part of life for our family than the average family, and it's something we discuss often in our home. I love coming home from work and telling my children about the new baby I was able to see born that day. When I was pregnant with my fourth child, I had a strong to desire to share my birth with my daughters.

To many, this may come across as extreme, bizarre, or even inappropriate. It wasn't an easy decision, and it's not an easy story to share. Most assume that children will be traumatized and scarred for life. This assumption is based on our own negative attitudes about birth; children have not formed their opinion yet and will only be scared by birth if the people around them are. In my heart, I knew that giving them the opportunity to see me give birth would help form their opinion on birth, its safety, and their ability to also give birth someday.

I invited them but gave them the choice to attend or not. I prepared them and talked openly about what it would be like. After many discussions and questions, they both decided to attend. They were frequently reminded that they could leave at any time. My mother-in-law was also present, and her role was to make sure the girls weren't disturbing me and that the birth wasn't too much for them to handle.

We woke the girls around 5:30 a.m., shortly before we left for the hospital. At first, they didn't understand why I wasn't making them any breakfast. At the hospital, they sat quietly and colored in a chair close to me. They took walks with Grandma when they were bored (yes, bored, not traumatized), and kissed my cheeks between contractions. I loved having them there. It kept me centered, and I felt so loved. I knew that by giving them the experience to watch a peaceful birth, they could take that memory with them forever. I hope they remember their mother's strength, control, and ability to give birth. I hope they carry that strength with them into their own births.

When their baby brother was born, I heard cheers of, "He's here! He's here!" They even cut the cord together! It was so exciting, and they were thrilled. Several minutes later, when we were all snuggling and admiring our new little prince, I asked my young daughters (ages six and seven and a half) if they had a good feeling inside. They both did. We talked about how that was the Holy Ghost and how God had blessed our family. We have remembered that day and remembered how we felt as I continue to teach them to recognize the Spirit. (See Appendix E for more about how my daughters felt.)

Having children attend a birth is a personal decision, and it isn't the right decision for everyone. But for us it was. No matter how you choose to talk to your children about birth, remember what you say will leave a strong impact on them and their perception.

I refuse to perpetuate negativity regarding birth (and all women's roles), especially regarding my daughters. They will get enough negativity from the world. From me they will receive an optimism based on truth and faith in God.

It is also important to teach our daughters that there is nothing shameful or immodest about giving birth. My girls laughed hysterically when I told them that I would be at least partially naked during the birth of their brother. Later on they asked me why it was okay for me to be naked then. This discussion can seem confusing to a child, especially when we've made efforts to teach them modest attitudes and behaviors, but it is an invaluable opportunity to discuss when certain things are appropriate and when they are not—not to mention an excellent time to discuss the sacredness and the miraculous design of the body.

A friend of mine once told me that her own mother allowed her to attend the birth of her youngest brother. At the time she was just ten years old, and she remembers feeling the Spirit stronger than she ever had up to that point in her life. She also told me that to this day, it is still one of the most spiritual experiences she has ever had. (Her inspiring story is what initially inspired me to invite my daughters to my birth.) How do you think this has shaped her opinion of childbirth? Compare that to a girl whose mother told her how horrible or painful or scary childbirth is. Which girl do you think will grow up to have the better opinion of birth?

If young women had more opportunities to see the positive, safe, and spiritual sides of childbirth, they would not fear birth so greatly when it is their turn to become mothers. Lack of positivity is a poison in the birthing world today. It has taken a miraculous event and made us fear it. It is seen as an inappropriate topic. But we can change all that. In one generation, it could be gone.

"Following a lengthy and heartfelt sacrament meeting discourse by a new father, drawing a detailed analogy between the beauties of childbirth and those of spiritual birth, the bishop of the ward rose to the pulpit and closed the meeting with, "I'm sure you all will join with me in appreciation of our speaker. We would like to thank him for his fine delivery."[1]

Steve and Kathy Anderson

Chapter 11

A Husband's Guide to Supporting and Protecting His Family

Husbands, you have the amazing ability to make your wife believe in herself. Your influence is most likely stronger than anyone else's influence in her life, and your opinion of her means more to her than anyone else's opinion. Your belief in her can and will give her the extra support she needs to achieve her highest of goals.

Long before I ever started writing this book, my husband and I were playing a game of MASH (a childish game that "predicts" the future). It was something we did to entertain ourselves (because we were broke) when we were living in Logan, Utah, both going to school, and had our whole lives ahead of us. During that time we had no idea where life would take us, so we amused ourselves with this nostalgic game.

On this particular day the game revealed to us that I would someday be a writer. I laughed so hard since I was majoring in music therapy and had never once actually considered writing a book. My husband turned and looked at me and said, "You could totally write a book; you are so passionate!" I was beyond flattered by the compliment. At first I thought he was just being nice, but upon further questioning I discovered that he actually saw the potential in me. (Prepare yourself: there will be a lot of gloating about my guy in this section!)

Fast forward several years later on a long drive for a family vacation. We were amusing ourselves with another daydream: What would our million-dollar idea be? By now I was deeply immersed in the field of childbirth and, like my husband had attributed to me earlier, quite passionate about it. I threw out the idea of writing a book about childbirth and spirituality. (Now, I don't really want to make a million dollars off of this book, but that is not the point of the story.) After saying my idea out loud, I quickly remembered my husband telling me that he thought I could write a book, and voila, I started writing that very night.

I didn't have my laptop or anything to write on with me. We stopped at the grocery store and I bought a *paper* tablet and a green pen. After I got our daughters to bed for the night, I opened up the empty tablet and began writing down every idea that had flooded into my mind since the car ride. My mom teased me the next morning, saying she could hear me frantically turning the pages all night. And now here you are reading it—all because my husband believed in me.

When a woman is in labor, she is easily influenced. She is working so hard and concentrating so intently that it is difficult for her to know what she is thinking. When someone tells her she is doing a great job, that she is in control, and that she is amazing, she will start thinking those things. But when her support person is not supportive or involved, she is left alone with her thoughts, fears, and fatigue. One mention of pain medication from an outside source sends her the message that she is inadequate. Husbands, you literally can make or break a birthing experience.

Up until the nineteen seventiess, husbands were not involved, or even allowed, in the birthing experience. With recent cultural changes, men are now not only allowed to be present during the birth, but are often expected to be their wife's rock, cheerleader, doula, and supporter. For the majority of men, supporting a woman though a birth goes against their nature. Men are fixers, yet a husband cannot step in and "fix" a birth. Birth requires a patient and supportive approach that allows labor to progress naturally, especially when labor is going slowly. This not only goes against a man's nature, but can make men feel helpless, and can give them plenty of time to get nervous and worry.

In order to fulfill new cultural expectations, men now have to learn enough about childbirth to understand how to fulfill their role of protector and supporter. Yet most men do not innately know how to support a birth, and are often expecting their wife's birth to be much different than it really will be. Hollywood (America's most used and worst birth resource!) does a horrible job of portraying birth. In Hollywood every birth is frantic. Women commonly yell things like "I hate you!" and "You did this to me," sending a message to men that their wives will have not only have fast births, but will also have a horrible birthing experience and blame it directly on the husband.

In reality, most births are not frantic. There is almost always plenty of time to get to the hospital or birth center. Typically, there is no rushing about or yelling. Women are not furious at their husbands, but are looking to them for emotional support, strength, and encouragement. Men are prepared for stressful, loud, and fast births, when most births are nothing of the sort. Most births are long, even boring for a support person.

This chapter is written to help you husbands learn how to protect, support, and love your wife during her pregnancy and birthing experience. I have worried about sounding like a lecturer, but I know my husband appreciates clear, no-hints communication. So consider this next section as a "honey-do" list to help you be a great spouse to your pregnant wife.

1. Walk hand-in-hand with your wife as she prepares to give birth. That includes—but is not limited to—attending childbirth education classes, reading birthing books, watching birth films, and reading birth blogs. (Shopping and helping set up baby items with interest and enthusiasm will get you a lot of brownie points too!)

2. Perform your preparatory duties willingly and with true interest.

3. Gain your own testimony of natural childbirth. You can't support her in something you don't believe in yourself.

4. Encourage her to practice her labor techniques beforehand and practice often with her. After all, you are the one required to remember everything, not her; she has enough to think about while she is in labor. (Unless you hire a doula. [See Appendix F] Then your doula can remember everything, tell you what to do, and make you look amazing to your wife!)

5. Love your wife enough to tune out *everything* while she is in labor. No texting, no getting bored, no talking about how tired or hungry or uncomfortable you are. (And definitely don't watch TV.)

6. Remind her of her goals while she is in labor. While it is tempting to encourage her to get an epidural so you both can rest and

feel relaxed, it is most helpful to remind her why she wanted to avoid intervention. Many women just need to be reminded, encouraged, and physically supported. You must stay strong and keep her on the path that you both know is most likely to bring you the most joy and the best outcome.

7. Be flexible if needed. Some women will swear they won't ask for an epidural but then end up wanting one after all. If you have reminded her of her pre-birth goals, offered support, and tried a different comfort measure, but she still says she wants an epidural, then she has changed her mind. Allow her to change it without making her feel judged or feel like a failure. It's not often, but sometimes the husband is more desirous of a natural birth than the wife is. Should you be in this position, allow her to choose the birth that will be most satisfying to her; it will have a longer lasting effect on her life than yours.

8. Remember that you and your wife are in charge, not the medical staff. You can ask for several minutes to process your options and make a prayerful decision in privacy.

9. Know her birth plan and step in if a medical professional tries to change the birth plan without your wife's consent.

10. Remember that this day should be focused on her and how amazing and strong she is.

11. Stay close to the Spirit during your child's birth. You may need to make difficult decisions and rely on the Lord for direction.

Things to remember *after* the baby is born:

1. While you both may be exhausted from a long labor, remember that she is more tired than you are and worked harder than you did. When men complain about how spent they feel after a delivery (even though they may not be drawing a comparison in their mind to the exertions of their wives), women usually feel unsupported. Your wife may feel like you don't understand what she just went through. Even if you were awake for forty-eight hours, missed five meals, and had a finger broken during her delivery, she still feels worse than you do and wants you to praise her for the amazing work she has done.

2. Understand the enormous value of breastfeeding (better health for baby, more oxytocin for mom, better recovery, and monetary savings, to name a few). Breastfeeding doesn't always come easy, but if nothing else, it's important to her and therefore important to you. If things aren't going well, don't immediately turn to the easy solution: bottles. Encourage her, assist her, and believe in her. For the first couple weeks of our first child's life, my husband got up with me every time I nursed the baby. He helped me find a good nursing position, would help me correct our daughter's latch, and helped me stay awake. He had taken a breastfeeding class with me prior to our daughter's arrival and in turn, he was able to be a great help to me!

3. Learn the signs of postpartum depression (see Appendix C), and make sure your wife gets the support she needs if she is experiencing it. If suddenly you no longer enjoy being around your wife because her personality has changed so much since having the baby, you need to pull closer to her and find resources on how to help her recover.

4. Most important, be a full partner as often as possible in caring for the baby. Change a diaper (or a lot of diapers), take over on a bad night, and let your wife know that her work in the home is invaluable.

Be There

During labor, just being close to your wife can mean the world to her. You may want to fix the problem. You want to take away the pain or offer something that will at least lessen it. Some women will not want much physical support, and some women may respond better to a doula than they do to their husbands. (Don't take it personally; doulas have a lot more practice.) But she will know if you are present. And I mean *really* present—physically, emotionally, and spiritually. If all you have is proximity, it doesn't count. You have to really be *with* her.

Picture yourself supporting your wife through a contraction that lasts sixty seconds, and then waiting for several minutes for the next contraction to come. This will go on for several hours, at least. There is a lot of down time, especially for first time birthers.

It is during this downtime that support people (not just husbands) are tempted to check Facebook, send a text or check the score of the big game. But doing so makes a woman feel unsupported. It is natural to think that since the woman isn't contracting that she no longer needs support. But women need just as much support in between contractions as they do during. In between contractions a woman needs to regroup emotionally in order to have the strength to continue on physically.

As spouses, being equally yoked is beneficial during birth. And while a man can't physically yoke himself to the birth, he can emotionally yoke himself. He can stay present during and in between contractions. During contractions, husbands can provide massages and verbal encouragement. In between contractions they can remind the woman how well she is doing, and tell her how proud he is of her. But when support people, such as the husband, emotionally unyoke in between contractions, laboring moms feel left alone and like the people around them don't care about what she is going through. When a man stays emotionally yoked in between contractions, his wife will feel supported and validated. This will help her stay emotionally strong, which will lead to greater physical endurance. Supporting your wife emotionally will strengthen her physically and emotionally.

During our fourth pregnancy, my husband and I decided not to hire a doula for our birth. We felt that by now, we could handle the situation alone. My husband is about as close to a doula as a man can get. He knows where to rub my back, what playlist to turn on, and exactly what to say. After giving birth three times already, I also had mastered my relaxation and breathing. I didn't need as much outside support. But I needed him to be with me during each and every contraction. Just knowing that he was there beside me made all the difference. I didn't feel alone. And even though he couldn't take the burden away from me, he walked beside me while I bore it. Supporting your wife this way will bring a new and unique bond to your marriage. It will also help you feel closer to your child. While it may be tempting to check out emotionally, resist the temptation. The last thing you want to do is make your wife feel like she is doing this by herself.

Protect

Staying emotionally yoked and protecting your wife from unnecessary intervention are the two most important things you can do during the birth of your child. There can be much to protect your wife from in the birthing room. Protecting your wife from an unwanted, unsupported, or traumatic birthing experience is no easy task. There is no other time where your wife will be so vulnerable and need you so intensely.

It is human nature to want to protect our loved ones from pain. Seeing your wife in pain from contractions may be difficult for you. You have to remember that the pain is not harmful to your wife's body. Many husbands encourage their wives to receive pain medication because they don't know what else to do and because they can't bear to see her hurting. While this is filled with good intentions, it doesn't provide any type of protection. It actually opens the door to possible risks. (See Appendix B.)

You may even need to protect her from herself. At 3:00 a.m. when she starts doubting herself and wants an epidural, you have to be strong enough to remind her why she didn't want one before labor started. Even though you are tired, frustrated, scared, and whatever else, you need to stay strong for her and for your child.

As a doula, I often feel like I work with husbands more than wives. When a woman is giving birth she often focuses internally and keeps conversation to a minimum. The person I communicate with the most is the dad. We are a team. We have one goal, and that goal is to support the mom. As a doula I can do much to help a woman have a natural birth, but there is one big restriction: I absolutely cannot tell a doctor what to do.

A dad, on the other hand, can say whatever he wants. It is dad's responsibility to watch everything that is going on and intervene if something goes against his wife's desire. You are your wife's voice. But many men feel like they can't speak up. Something about being in a hospital makes people feel like they are back in third grade and the obstetrician is the principal. In reality, *you* are in charge. You are the one paying the obstetrician to safely support you through this journey.

Should you see your wife being treated poorly or see other people making decisions for her, it is your responsibility to speak up and ensure her physical and emotional safety. Interventions are commonplace in a hospital setting, and unless you have communicated your preferences, it may be assumed that you are fine with common interventions. As the protector, it's your role to step in at any time to protect your wife's wishes and ensure that any offered interventions are being used appropriately

Your goal is to keep your family safe in the delivery room, on the road, at the playground, everywhere. Fatherhood starts at conception, not the day you go home from the hospital. In the delivery room, the best chance for safety is to preserve a natural birth.

HELP YOUR WIFE FEEL SAFE AND SECURE

You should also do everything you can to make your wife feel safe, secure, accepted, and not judged. I once spoke with a woman whose husband made her feel self-conscious about giving birth. During their first pregnancy, they attended a childbirth education class. She told me about one night in particular when the class was watching a childbirth movie. As an educator, this night is always a little unpredictable for me because I never know how my class will react. Some classes are immature and laugh and snicker throughout to deal with their embarrassment. Other classes are very interested and find that watching the video makes them feel much more prepared.

The husband of the woman I mentioned wasn't handling the video well on this night. It showed the woman vocalizing a lot and moving around in a manner that seemed odd to him. He leaned over to her and said, "I really hope you don't act like that!"

As the birth on the film progressed, there were, of course, images of body parts we typically don't want our husbands looking at. Many couples do not feel uncomfortable watching a birth, and many couples do. This is a personal preference, and neither is right nor wrong. I always give my class members the option to watch or not. I provide the opportunity, should someone find it helpful. This particular husband was uncomfortable watching a birth. Instead of politely opting out of the viewing, he left and never came back to the class. This woman attended her final class alone.

This sent a strong message to the wife, who greatly desired a natural birth. She feared how her husband would view her or react to her while she was in labor. She was so nervous about doing something that would upset him that she opted for an epidural to protect herself from his reaction. This in turn robbed her of the birth she desired.

Your job is to make your wife feel safe enough to labor in any way that she chooses. Judging her will only interfere with her natural ability to birth. She needs to know that she can moan, move, and dress however she would like and that you will support her through it all. And if watching a birthing video is too much for you to cope with, just politely excuse yourself and let her learn from it. It is one thing for you to not want to watch. That is fine. But it is another to make your wife feel like if she acts a certain way, she is doing something wrong. When it comes to birth, there should be no shame and no fear of immodesty or anything else.

FACILITATE POSTPARTUM RECOVERY

Your wife may need extra protection once the baby is brought home as well, especially during the first six weeks while her body is recovering. Ensure that she is getting adequate rest and nutrition. Many new moms feel so tired and overwhelmed that they feel they don't have time to take care of themselves. If your baby fusses a lot at night, make sure and take part of the nighttime load, at least on the weekend (or nights you don't have to go to work the following morning).

Protect her from too many people coming over to "help" who are really only there to hold the baby. Moms shouldn't feel like they have to share their baby more than they are comfortable with. Grandmas, aunts, sisters, and friends should help by doing dishes, preparing meals, doing housework, running errands, and caring for older children. If you find that your wife is tidying up while everyone else is oohing and ahhing over your child, speak up! Let them know that your wife needs to rest and that she could use their help in other ways. Be sure that you are doing your part with the housework as well.

After I had my third child, my mom stayed with us for a week or two. We had a three- and a four-year-old at the time, and her presence made a huge difference in our lives. We needed her. I was able to take a nap with my new son each morning, and it meant so much to me to know that she was there to handle my other responsibilities for a while.

With each birth, both my mom and my husband's mom have been able to come and support us. If this is true for you, count your blessings. Show your appreciation to your mother or mother-in-law in words and deeds. And if you find it hard to get along with either your mother or your mother-in-law under one roof for an extended period of time, put the needs of your family first. Keep the peace and know that things would be harder without help from family. If you do not have family that is able or willing to help, you will need to do more to help your wife, especially if you can't take much time off from work. Coordinate with her friends or the Relief Society president to ensure that your wife isn't left unsupported.

SHOW YOUR LOVE

Most important, love your wife, your child, and your new life as a father. Your new life of parenting can take some time to adjust to, and it isn't always an easy transition. But cherish the time. Nothing will melt your wife's heart more than seeing you be a loving and gentle father.

Our oldest daughter cried so much when she was a baby. She would cry all night and all day, and there were times that both my husband and I thought we were going to lose our minds. He was getting his master's degree at the time and would often swaddle our daughter up nice and tight, and lay her beside his leg on the couch while he stayed up at night to do homework. Yes, he was exhausted, overwhelmed, stressed—and did I mention exhausted? But he loved our daughter, loved having her close to him. He knew the moments were fleeting, and if he was home, he wanted to be with her. And now, over nine years later, they still have an amazingly close relationship that fills our family with joy.

The best hours of sleep I ever got during that time period were the hours I knew she was snuggled up beside him on the couch. It put me at ease to know they were together and that if she needed me, he would bring her to me and I wouldn't even have to get out of bed. It sounds like a small thing, but it was a huge help. Sometimes I would be so tired from walking the halls trying to get her to go to sleep that my feet would start to ache the second they hit the floor when I got out of bed. I can't imagine getting through those few months without my husband's help.

Husbands, you truly have the power to influence your family for good. Seeing you walk through the door at the end of a long day will send relief surging through your wife. And while you may not want to be bombarded with a wife desperate for a shower, a crying baby, no dinner, and a messy house, remember that these phases pass quickly (and even more quickly when mom and dad can be a great team through them). Before you know it you will be bombarded with children smiling and cheering to see you pull up in the driveway. There may even come a time when you miss the simple chaos of just having one tiny baby.

RELY ON THE SPIRIT

Always remember that one of the most important things you can offer your wife during this time is your priesthood power. Use it to comfort, encourage, and support her during this time. I tend to be a high-stress

140

woman, and I rely on my husband's priesthood authority and closeness to the Spirit to help me distinguish between my own feelings of anxiety and actual spiritual promptings. It always brings me comfort to know that my husband is a worthy priesthood holder whom I can call on for a priesthood blessing whenever I need it. I know that he is in tune and that he will be prompted when needed. I will never forget receiving a blessing from him before we left for the hospital to have our first child. I was so prepared for that birth—way more prepared than the average first-time mom. But I was still nervous. After receiving my blessing I could feel the Spirit enter into our experience, and its calming presence was with me the entire time. Even when things became difficult and stressful, I could always take a moment to breathe and tune back into the Spirit that the blessing invited.

Just like your wife supports you in your priesthood role, return that support to her in her divine role to bring your children into this earthly realm. Help her reach her sacred potential.

You may come to a fork in the road during your wife's birth. It is important to be in tune with the Holy Ghost so that you can have the Lord's guidance should you need to make a difficult decision. You may go down a path that the two of you initially wanted to avoid. Being worthy and having faith will make it easy for you to make the best choice for your family.

Remember this counsel from Elder M. Russell Ballard:

> Fathers perform priesthood ordinances and give priesthood blessings, including father's blessings to their children. They pray for and with family members, collectively and individually. They set an example of respect and love for their eternal companion and mother of their children. In all things they follow the example of the Savior and strive to be worthy of His name and His blessing. Fathers should seek constantly for guidance from the Holy Ghost so they will know what to do, what to say, and also know what *not* to do and what *not* to say.
>
> Fathers are expected by God and His prophets not only to provide for their families, but also to protect them. Dangers of all sorts abound in the world in which we live. Physical protection against natural or man-made hazards is important. Moral dangers are also all around us, confronting our children from their early years. Fathers play a vital role in protecting children against such snares.

We know that a father's role does not end with presiding, providing and protecting family members. On a day to day basis, fathers can and should help with the essential nurturing and bonding associated with feeding, playing, storytelling, loving, and all the rest of the activities that make up family life.[2]

Your wife will always remember how you made her feel during this time in her life. By following the Savior's example of love and compassion, you will set yourself up for a lifetime of love and appreciation from your wife and children and approval from your Father in Heaven.

NOTES

1. Steve and Kathy Anderson, "After All," *Ensign*, November 1971.
2. M. Russell Ballard, "The Sacred Responsibility of Parenthood," from an Education Week devotional address given on August 19, 2003, at Brigham Young University.

Section Four
WORKSHEET

What types of emotions have you seen women around you experience after giving birth?

Describe how you hope to feel after you give birth.

What qualities do you see in your spouse that will help your marriage during your pregnancy and birth?

What are some things you can do now to prevent postpartum depression?

Who would you turn to for help if you felt you had postpartum depression?

List three things you can see yourself doing or saying to help a younger woman look forward to giving birth someday.

CONCLUSION

For more than a hundred years, our society's focus on birth has been, "how can we change or improve birth?" But for me, my focus has always been, "what can I learn about birth to help me better understand God's plan for birth?" This personal focus has not only strengthened my testimony but has also made giving birth and helping others during this experience one of the most meaningful events of my life. It has taught me to trust in the birthing process as I continue to put my trust in the Lord.

My motivation in writing this book was to help LDS women have more positive birthing experiences with better outcomes, and to give them the tools they need to make informed and inspired decisions. My prayer for each of you is that your births are not only safe and satisfying, but that they strengthen your testimony and help you feel God's love for you. I hope your birth strengthens your family values and love for your husband, as well as helps you see yourself in a new, powerful light. I hope it testifies of your divine role and ability to safely bring spirits to the earth. I hope giving birth fills your heart with love and gratitude, leaving you feeling more accomplished that you have ever been—more excited about the future, more devoted to the Lord than you have ever felt.

My own experience, research, and pondering have shown me that God designed birth a certain way to achieve certain outcomes. He loves you. Not only does He want you to create a family, but He also wants your family to thrive. He wants your birth to occur safely so your family can experience divinely designed blessings.

FINAL WORKSHEET

Aside from a healthy mom and a healthy baby, what is your number one goal for your birth?

What do you feel is the most important lesson to take from this book?

What is your next step in preparing for your birth?

Appendix A

WHAT'S IN A DUE DATE?

For decades, thirty-seven weeks has been considered full term. Because of this, many women feel like they should go into labor before their due date when, in reality, many babies are not ready to be born until well after their forty-week due date.[1] A due date is just an estimate, meaning it's the closest guess we can come up with. It is certainly not an expiration date!

ACOG has recently come out with new guidelines to help us understand due dates and has changed full term from thirty-seven weeks to thirty-nine weeks. Research teaches us there is a small number of babies that are ready to be born at or around thirty-seven weeks but that the vast majority of babies will need at least thirty-nine weeks, and some will need the full forty-two weeks.

Thirty-seven weeks: early term

Thirty-nine weeks: full term

Forty-one weeks: late term

Forty-two weeks: post term[2]

In low-risk situations, labor will begin when a fetus is ready to survive on its own and when a woman's body is ready to go through the birthing process. As an infant grows and develops during the pregnancy, the mother's body also changes to prepare to give birth. Many physical and hormonal (physiological) changes precede a birth. For example, the mother's cervix will soften and move forward to allow for dilation and descent of the infant, the baby will engage inside the mother's pelvis, and the mother's hormones will stimulate the onset of labor. Once everything is physically and physiologically lined up, labor begins. Remember: "You and your fetus/newborn have innate abilities to start labor, labor and give birth, breastfeed, and become deeply attached to one another. The ebbing and flowing of hormones drives these well organized, finely tuned processes."[3]

Except in rare cases, labor will begin on its own when both mom and baby are ready. There is not a worldwide epidemic of women never going into labor. Have faith; your day *will* come.

NOTES

1. "Definition of Term Pregnancy," *ACOG*, March 2014.
2. Ibid.
3. "Understanding & Navigating the Maternity Care System: Hormones Driving Labor and Birth," *Childbirth Connection*, April 2011.

Appendix B
BENEFITS AND RISKS GUIDE

he following is a quick overview of potential benefits and
potential risks surrounding typical birthing choices. Of course
there are gray areas and exceptions; because every body and
every birth is different, there are no blanket statements that cover *all*
births. However, it is easy to get into the trap of believing that you are the
exception. That kind of thinking has influenced the skyrocketing increase
in birth interventions. When picturing your birth, it would be most helpful to believe that your birth will be a low-risk experience and that you are
much more likely to fall under the umbrella of "normal." Do not assume
that your decisions will have consequences well outside of the norm. Also
keep in mind that even though statistics give percentages of occurrence,
your experience will only have one of two percentages: 0 percent and 100
percent, meaning that even if there is only a 25 percent chance that you
will experience a risk you want to avoid, should you experience it, you will
experience it at 100 percent. Understanding this helps you visualize what
it would actually mean to you should you end up with a risk you were
hoping to avoid, and helps you make decisions that will improve your
likelihood of avoiding certain scenarios.

When looking at these lists, it is easy to see that the only scenario
with more pros than cons is natural childbirth. While no pro or con is
guaranteed, you can safely assume that the more pros a list has, the more
likely you are to have a safe and positive experience. On the other hand,
the longer the list of cons, the more likely you are to experience something
undesirable.

POTENTIAL BENEFITS OF NATURAL CHILDBIRTH	POTENTIAL CONS OF NATURAL CHILDBIRTH
Safer for baby	Intimidating
Safer for mom	Tiring
Shorter labor	Fear of the unknown
Ability to move and change position	Pain
Ability to maintain agency during the birthing process	Intense, even overwhelming for some
Less likely for baby to experience fetal distress	
Increased production of endorphins for fighting pain	
Increased production of oxytocin to keep labor moving forward	
More likely that baby will be in optimal positioning for delivery	
Shorter pushing duration	
Less likely to require interventions like Pitocin, assisted delivery, or cesareans	
Heightened emotions at moment of birth	
More likely to experience feelings of intense bonding	
Quicker recovery for mom	
Timely lactogenesis	
More likely to breastfeed	
Less likely to experience postpartum depression	
More likely to be happy and satisfied with birthing experience	
Sense of accomplishment	
Feelings of joy and empowerment	
Increased faith and testimony building	

POTENTIAL BENEFITS OF EPIDURAL PAIN MANAGEMENT	POTENTIAL RISKS OF EPIDURAL PAIN MANAGEMENT
Pain relief	Longer labor
Time to rest	Decreased production of oxytocin, resulting in fewer contractions
	Decrease of contractions, leading to Pitocin use
	Inadequate pain relief
	Spinal headache
	Inability to change positions
	Inability to control future decisions
	Increased likelihood of fetal distress
	Increased likelihood of assisted delivery
	Increased likelihood of cesarean birth
	Prolonged pushing
	Increased likelihood for vaginal injury
	More likely that baby will be in poor position for delivery
	Lack of oxytocin at birth, often resulting in decreased bonding
	Dulled newborn reflexes
	Delayed lactogenesis
	Difficulty breastfeeding
	Longer recovery for mom
	Increased likelihood of postpartum depression
	Decreased birth satisfaction
	Though unlikely, epidurals have been associated with long–term nerve damage, depressed respiration, cardiac arrest, and even maternal death

POTENTIAL BENEFITS OF PITOCIN INDUCTION	POTENTIAL RISKS OF PITOCIN INDUCTION
Ability to start labor when necessary due to health concerns for mom or baby Ability to start labor when mom is past forty-two weeks gestation	No guarantee that labor will start No production of endorphins or oxytocin Contractions are more painful, longer, closer together, and dilate the cervix slower than natural contractions More likely to receive pain medication Increased likelihood of fetal distress Increased likelihood of assisted delivery or cesarean birth Increased likelihood of premature birth Dulled newborn reflexes Lack of oxytocin at birth, often resulting in decreased bonding Difficulty breastfeeding Decreased birth satisfaction

Appendix C
BIRTH PREFERENCES QUIZ

his quiz is designed to help you figure out which type of birth and which type of care provider is most appealing to you. There are no right or wrong answers. Read each statement and determine if the statement is "true, false, or neutral," based on your personal opinion, Then, add up your points and find out which type of birth you will prefer.

STATEMENT	TRUE	FALSE	NEUTRAL
I trust in my body's ability to give birth.	0	2	1
I trust that an OB/GYN would only offer interventions when truly needed.	2	0	1
I do not like hospitals, nor do I like being a medical patient.	0	2	1
I will be disappointed if I do not have a natural birth.	0	2	1
I would like a natural birth, but am okay receiving an epidural if my labor is long and difficult.	1	0	1
Breastfeeding is extremely important to me.	0	2	1
I would feel unsafe giving birth in a location that is unable to accommodate cesareans.	2	0	1
I would feel safer giving birth in a location that does not have birth interventions available.	0	2	1
Having optimal amounts of oxytocin during my birth is very important to me.	0	2	1
I am not afraid of childbirth.	0	2	1
When I picture myself giving birth, I feel nervous and worry about how painful or difficult it could be.	2	0	1
I am proactively preparing to give birth.	0	2	1
I do not have much time for or interest in preparing for birth.	2	0	1
Natural birth feels intimidating, but I am interested in having it as a goal because of health benefits for myself and my baby.	1	2	0

I want to experience childbirth.	0	0	1
Even knowing the risks of cesarean birth, it feels less scary than natural birth.	2	2	1
I am hoping to have a large family.	0	0	1
In my everyday life, I try to avoid using medications and prefer to use natural remedies.	0	0	1
I have healthy self-esteem.	0	0	1
I have a good relationship with my spouse, and know that he will be an important part of the birth.	0	0	1
I have faith that Heavenly Father will make up for my human shortcomings during childbirth.	0	0	1
I feel honored to have the opportunity to give birth.	0	0	1
To me, natural birth is worth the effort, even if my labor is long and difficult, because of the physical and emotional benefits.	0	0	1
To me, natural birth is something women do to boost their egos, and does not appear to be better than a medical birth.	2	2	1
Even if I truly need an intervention, part of me will still be disappointed for receiving it.	0	0	1
I feel that birth interventions are modern day miracles, and I am thankful I don't have to experience natural birth.	2	2	1

IF YOU SCORED 0 TO 18: A natural birth is important to you physically, emotionally, and even spiritually. You view birth as an important event in your life and one that will have long lasting effects on your future. You look forward to your birth not just because it will make you a mother but also because you feel it will be an amazing and uplifting experience. You would probably appreciate the midwifery model of care, and may even opt for an out-of-hospital birth.

THINGS TO REMEMBER: Your worth is not determined by your birth. Remain flexible and open to changes in your birth plan should things take a turn you were hoping to avoid.

IF YOU SCORED 20 TO 34: You are a middle-of-the road woman and will probably be fine with either type of birth, as long as you feel like the decisions regarding your birth were based on truth. You would do well with an obstetrician or a midwife. You would like to have a natural birth but will not be disappointed if you do not have one.

THINGS TO REMEMBER: Being too laidback can hand over the agency of your birth to someone else. Stay present during decision-making so you don't leave the experience wondering if you should have done something differently.

IF YOU SCORED 36 TO 52: Natural birth is not a priority for you, and you may be planning on receiving certain interventions. You would feel more comfortable with an obstetrician and will definitely want to give birth in a hospital. For you, birth is a means to an end.

THINGS TO REMEMBER: Even if you don't want a natural birth, it doesn't guarantee that you will be happy with a medical birth. Remember that signing up for one intervention can often mean signing up for two or three. Make sure that your choices are still made with the goal of optimal health. Remain close to the Spirit during important decision-making times.

Appendix D

*B*elow is a handout that I received from a friend of mine who is a counselor specialized in postpartum depression. I encourage all of my clients to assess themselves once a month for the first year of their baby's life.

COULD I HAVE POSTPARTUM DEPRESSION?

Do you . . .

Have trouble sleeping?

Find you're exhausted?

Notice a decrease in your appetite?

Worry about little things that never used to bother you?

Wonder if you'll ever have time to yourself again?

Think your children would be better off without you?

Worry that your husband will get tired of you feeling this way?

Snap at your husband and children over everything?

Think everyone else is a better mother than you are?

Cry over the slightest thing?

No longer enjoy the things you used to enjoy?

Isolate yourself from your friends and neighbors?

Fear leaving the house or being alone?

Have anxiety attacks?

Have unexplained anger?

Have difficulty concentrating?

Think something else is wrong with you or your marriage?

Feel like you will always feel this way and never get better?

Many new mothers will experience some of these feelings. If you answered yes to more than three of these questions, you may have postpartum depression (PPD). PPD affects 20 to 30 percent of all postpartum women. It is a real illness. It is treatable. Do not deny yourself the opportunity to feel good again. Do not let misinformation, uncertainty, shame, finances, embarrassment, or denial get in the way of you getting the help you need. Talk to your doctor. Talk to your husband or partner. Once you decide to seek treatment, you will be on the road to feeling better.

Courtesy of the Postpartum Stress Center: postpartumstress.com

Appendix E

Shortly after attending the birth of her little brother, my daughter, Magdalen, wrote the following story. She was six years old at the time. (She even came in second place in a state-wide writing competition!)

BIRTH: A MAGICAL MOMENT

When Brandon was born I felt excited.

I woke up early to go to the hospital.

Grandma took me to the playroom, and I remember drawing when I was bored.

The room was dark, and there was calm music.

I remember my mom trying really hard to get him out.

I remember his head poking out.

The umbilical cord was on his tummy, and I cut off the umbilical cord.

I was excited to cut it!

Brandon was crying. LOUD!

I really was wanting to hold him.

I was excited to hold him, but he started to cry.

I'm glad I was there.

It was a magical moment.

Appendix F

Research[1] shows that doula support provides a

- 31 percent decrease in the use of Pitocin
- 28 percent decrease in the risk of C-section
- 34 percent decrease in the risk of being dissatisfied with the birth experience
- 14 percent decrease in the risk of newborns being admitted to NICU
- 12 percent increase in the likelihood of a spontaneous vaginal birth
- 9 percent decrease in the use of any medications for pain relief

There are skilled and talented doulas all across the United States, and many of them are members of The Church of Jesus Christ of Latter-day Saints, who not only believe that God divinely designed childbirth but are also familiar with this book and are eager to help you have a sacred and safe birthing experience. If you would like to learn more about the doulas in your area, visit www.mariebigelow.com/sacredgiftsdoulas.

NOTES

1. Ellen D. Hodnett et al., "Continuous Support for Women During Childbirth (Review)," *PubMed*, 2013.

ACKNOWLEDGMENTS

*F*irst, I'd like to thank my parents, Bron and Valerie Ingoldsby, for giving me a wonderful childhood, teaching me the importance of the family, and always supporting and encouraging me. My twin sister, Hilary, for being my biggest fan in all that I do, and my closest friend, always. I want to thank my cheerleaders—Todd Bigelow, Hilary Whitesides, Emily Perry, Jen Dunn, Jenna Dayton, Laura Brotherson, Lesli Spiers, Nicki Hope, and Jane Johnson—who tolerated years of childbirth discussions, allowed me to bounce ideas off of them, and kept me going when I really wanted to give up. My editors—Hilary Ingoldsby Whitesides, Lesli Speirs, Amanda Lewis, Breanna Bennett Olaveson, and Kimiko Christensen Hammari—for helping me organize my thoughts and perfect my message. And thank you to everyone at Cedar Fort who believed in this project, and helped turned my vision into a reality.

I also need to thank all of the couples who have attended my childbirth education classes and those whose births I have attended. It is an honor to be a part of someone else's journey to parenthood, and each of you have touched my life and taught me over and over again just how important birth is. To Christina Howell, for not only being my doula, but for taking me under your wing and teaching me how to be a doula.

And most important, to my ever-supportive husband, Todd. I have always known that being married to a doula is not easy . . . for many reasons! I think being married to a doula who also wants to write a book has got to be brutal! Thank you for picking up the slack when I am at a birth, for believing in me, for having low expectations at dinnertime, for laughing when I'm sitting in my pajamas in front of the computer at 4 p.m., for countless hours of listening to me talk about my ideas, for holding me when I cried, for helping me find the motivation to continue, and for putting up with me as I have spent years working on this project! I know it wasn't always easy, and I couldn't have done it without you. You truly have made all of my dreams come true. You have helped me continue to grow into the person I want to be, and have been my partner as we have built our own home and beautiful family. I love you!

ABOUT THE AUTHOR

*M*arie-Ange Bigelow's fascination with childbirth began when she was a teenager taking voice lessons. Her voice teacher had just given birth and compared delivering her child to singing a high note and holding it for a long time. Over the next decade Marie found a way to combine her love of music and her interest in childbirth as she graduated magna cum laude with a bachelor's degree in Music Therapy, and then went on to specialize in Music Therapy Assisted Childbirth. Marie also became a certified doula and childbirth educator, and was recently awarded the prestigious Advanced Doula Designation. Marie has not only helped couples prepare for birth through her popular childbirth classes, but has supported hundreds of parents during the births of their children in hospitals, birth centers, and homes.

Marie is passionate about childbirth and positive outcomes for mothers and infants. It was this passion, along with her belief that women should be empowered by knowledge and gospel truths, that led her to write *The Sacred Gift of Childbirth: Making Empowered Choices for You and Your Baby.*

Along with her own childbirth-centered blog, Marie's work has been featured in *International Doula* and on popular websites such as TheMommyMethed.education.com, SheKnows.com, and Parents.com. Marie and her husband, Todd, are enjoying raising their four beautiful children in Boise, Idaho. As a family they enjoy biking, traveling, music, and movie nights.

To read more about Marie, visit www.mariebigelow.com.